SACRIFICE

Based on the proceedings of a
Conference on Sacrifice held at Cumberland Lodge, Windsor, England
from February 23rd to 25th, 1979

SACRIFICE

Edited by

M.F.C. Bourdillon
Department of Sociology
University of Zimbabwe, Salisbury
Zimbabwe

Meyer Fortes
Cambridge University
England

 1980

Published by Academic Press
for the Royal Anthropological Institute of
Great Britain and Ireland

ACADEMIC PRESS
A Subsidiary of Harcourt Brace Jovanovich, Publishers

ACADEMIC PRESS INC. (LONDON) LTD.
24/28 Oval Road,
London NW1

United States Edition published by
ACADEMIC PRESS INC.
111 Fifth Avenue
New York, New York 10003

British Cataloguing in Publication Data
Sacrifice
1. Lord's Supper – Congresses
2. Atonement – Congresses
I. Bourdillon, M.F.C.
II. Fortes, Meyer   III. Royal Anthropological
Institute
234   BV825.2   80-40424
ISBN 0-12-119040-4

Printed in Great Britain by
John Wright & Sons Ltd at the Stonebridge Press, Bristol

PREFACE

Anthropologists and Theologians: Common Interests and Divergent Approaches

Meyer Fortes

What is it that anthropologists and theologians have in common, by way of discipline or by way of 'problematic', that makes possible the kind of exchange recorded in this volume; and, contrariwise, in what ways do their interests and techniques of inquiry diverge? Michael Bourdillon's *Introduction* offers a balanced answer to these questions, one that only someone as equally at home in both camps as he is could provide. Is there anything left for a mere, one-sided social anthropologist to add? Listening to these papers and the discussions at the conference, I found myself sometimes impressed by the way in which the theologians and the anthropologists were arguing from a common ground, and at other times struck by the divergencies, even the contradictions, between their approaches and aims.

No topic in the field of their shared concern with religious institutions and values brings out these alternatives so clearly as does sacrifice. For there is no ritual institution as central to all but a minority of both the scriptural and the non-scriptural religions of mankind. And the alternatives emerge in the ways all the key concepts common to both disciplines are used—concepts such as 'symbol', 'myth', 'belief', 'meaning' etc. Not that there is unanimity of usage or definition in either camp; but granted the grey areas of ambiguity on both sides, the differences are clear enough. They are frankly indicated in Bourdillon's *Introduction*, most precisely when he contrasts what he describes as the 'embarrassed silence' of anthropologists on 'the relationship between the effects of rituals and what participants expect to achieve through them', with how theologians regard this relationship. 'Theologians' he continues 'are part of the tradition they study and must be convinced that their rituals have the effects that they want them to have'. In other words, I would suggest, being in part actors in their own religious systems, theologians must *believe*, whereas anthropologists, I would argue, who are primarily observers, cannot but be *agnostic* if they want to achieve objectivity.

To make my point clearer, let me look back thirty years to a celebrated lecture by Evans-Pritchard (1950). Inaugurating in 1948 the annual lecture series at Exeter College, Oxford dedicated to the memory of Rector R. R. Marett, he bluntly accused his fellow anthropologists and even the founding fathers of being incapable of understanding the religions of non-western people. The reason, he claimed, was that they were themselves irreligious or even atheistic. It was a strange shaft to launch in a lecture commemorating the scholar who particularly emphasised the 'sacramental' features of primitive religion—and who, incidentally, was the only British anthropologist cited by the theologian Rudolf Otto in his influential book *Das Heilige* (English translation by J. W. Harvey, 1950); and, let me add that Otto's concept of the numinous as the awe-evoking character of the Holy, appealed in its turn to Marett and indeed met with approval from Evans-Pritchard (1956: 8).

With few exceptions the anthropological community rejected Evans-Pritchard's accusation. Had Tylor, Frazer, Marett, Malinowski, Radcliffe-Brown, and Evans-Pritchard himself, in his already famous book on Zande witchcraft, not made fundamental contributions to the study of the religions of mankind? Tylor, indeed, writing at a time when the intellectual climate was still dominated by the bitter Victorian confrontation between the world view of science and the teachings of theology, ends his great book on *Primitive Culture* with a call for co-operation between anthropologists and theologians (1871 Vol. 2: 449ff).

But there was and there remains a point to Evans-Pritchard's complaint. There is no doubt that most of our illustrious predecessors and we, their successors, were and are, to say the least, agnostic in their and our *professional* attitudes to religion. Moreover, I doubt if any of our famous forebears referred to above, were believing adherents of any theistic, animistic, or other form of cult ordered to doctrines of supernatural powers. And this is certainly the case also with many if not most social anthropologists of Evans-Pritchard's generation. Nor are anthropologists alone in this. The same can be said of sociologists and psychologists engaged in the study of religious systems. It is significant that Durkheim and Mauss, those eloquent lapsed Jewish social philosophers, and their followers, were frankly atheistic; yet it was to their studies of primitive religion that Evans-Pritchard himself turned with admiration for sociological inspiration.

Let me emphasise that what I am here concerned with is not the personal religious beliefs and commitments of anthropologists, but the standpoint that I think is required of them for a professionally correct approach to their task. Nor do I think that this represents a peculiar or sinister value bias. What I am saying is that it is only to the extent to which an anthropologist is able to maintain an agnostic point of view about the beliefs and practices he is examining that he can achieve objectivity in his understanding and presentation of these beliefs and practices. And objectivity, in the sense of analysis and description that are accepted as valid by reason of their compatibility with comparative evidence and the independent observations and analyses of other qualified enquirers in the same field, is, surely, a *sine qua non* for all anthropological scholarship.

This, as I see it, is where the critical distinction lies between anthropologists and theologians—or rather, between an anthropological approach and a theological approach. For, as Bourdillon reminds us, there are theologians who can and do adopt a specifically anthropological approach in their studies even of their own religious beliefs and institutions. (A fine example is that of the late E. O. James). And more specific, of course, to our interests, are the contributions of such famous 'applied theologians' as Codrington, Junod, Edwin Smith, Westermann, Bryant and many other missionaries whose ethnographic researches have so incomparably enriched our study. Conversely,there are anthropologists, *pace* Evans-Pritchard, who themselves belong to theistic or other supernaturally-directed cults, and who frankly approach their studies from the standpoint of their religious values. And as for the agnostic anthropologists, borrowing concepts and categories from theological scholarship is as common among them as the reverse influence is among theologians.

Evans-Pritchard, as it happens, nicely documents the distinction I have in mind. In his study of Zande witchcraft (1937), the stance which gives this great work its scholarly and scientific authority is that of an agnostic observer judging Zande beliefs and practices by criteria of Western, scientifically-shaped concepts of causality, human nature, and natural laws. In contrast, in *Nuer Religion*, the work which inspired the renewed attention of anthropologists to the institution of sacrifice that is exemplified in our Symposium, his position is almost the reverse. The brilliant ethnography is organised in terms of a model derived from such theoretical sociologists as Hubert and Mauss. But it is also shot through with indirect witness to Evans-Pritchard's personal theistic religious commitment, as Horton and Finnegan suggest (1973: 45—6) and with evidence, in his terminology of description and his interpretative scheme, of his borrowings from theological and Biblical scholarship. It is of interest to contrast Monica Wilson's studies of Nyakyusa witchcraft and religion (1951; 1956). The Christian principles and ideals for which she is well-known are not obtruded into these studies but are drawn upon in separate, deliberately evaluated contexts (as e.g. 1971).

Let us look more closely at the distinction I am making. Logically speaking, from a theological point of view, there can be no questioning the reality or the actuality of the existence 'out there', independently of the existence of Mankind, of such supernatural power or powers in any religious system. This holds for all religious systems, not only for 'revealed' religions of Judaeo-Christian origin. Such postulates (as an observer would put it) though not always in the form of a conception of a single, omnipotent, omniscient and absolute creator/deity or cosmic force, have been reported for most human societies. Whether or not the Nuer conception of *Kwoth*, or the Dogon *Amma*, or the Akan *Nyame*, and other such African concepts can properly be identified with the Judaeo-Christian concept of God, is not the significant issue. What I am getting at is the assumption, from the actor's point of view, the faith, that the super-natural powers or agencies postulated in his religious system, be they or it deity, divinity, ancestor spirits, nature spirits etc., do really exist, and the corollary is that they can be known and experienced cognitively, affectively, instrumentally, and morally by virtue, *inter alia*, of their (its, his) intervention in human affairs. The Nuer claim to know that *Kwoth* exists because they get ill, among other things, and according to them they are able to show, for instance by divination as well as by the effects of their rituals, that this is due to the intervention of *Kwoth* in their life. The Tallensi reason in the same way about their ancestors; and Tikopia, like many other peoples, including some with scriptural religions, claim to have evidence of the reality of their divinities or their ancestors when mediums or seers become possessed.

'If no effect of God can ever be discerned then in effect God is nowhere . . .' comments Bowker (1973: 84) in the course of his profound and learned study of the very issue I am here considering; and he adds that 'all theistic traditions have at some point suggested discernible (claimed) effects of God . . .' A Nuer or Dogon or Akan theologian would agree with reference to the supernatural powers they acknowledge. And they would associate with this the same implications as arise in scriptural religions, namely, that there is an inescapable obligation on the part of mankind to show their sense of their dependence on these supernatural powers by their conduct, and especially in the performance of rituals which, in their eyes, testify to the existence and the powers of these agencies.

It is not relevant to my purpose to go into questions of a general theoretical kind regarding the nature of ritual. I use the term to refer to any customary spoken and/or acted out pattern of behaviour recognised by the actors as directed towards or referring to the supernatural, or as I prefer to say occult powers and agencies (Fortes, 1966). I see ritual as from the actor's point of view a customary activity of necessity specialised for the task of relating Man's cognisable world of tangible, ponderable, visible and controllable mundane existence—the profane world of Durkheimian sociology—to the intangible, imponderable, invisible, uncontrollable, uncognisable world of non-material powers and forces assumed and believed by him to exist in a different, not otherwise accessible sphere of reality—the Durkheimian sacred. And sacrifice is such a ritual *par excellence*.

As all the papers in our symposium—and most notably Audrey Hayley's—show, for the believer, and therefore for the theologian, his ritual acts are perceived as being efficacious in relation to the occult in as real a sense for its context as is any technical action in relation to the actor's material world.[1] Sacrifice, from the believer's point of view, is intended and expected *really* to expiate his sin, *really* to propitiate his God or other divinities, *really* to erase mystical pollution, *really* to conduce towards, if not necessarily to succeed in removing his affliction. And the culminating communion of sharing the consumption of the sacrifice with the recipient supernatural agencies marks the transaction as an affirmation of an on-going relationship of mutuality between givers and receivers of the sacrifice.

The common meal as distinct from the communion rite that so often rounds off the sacrificial act may well be, to the observer and in some cases even to the actor, its most significant and most intelligible sociological aspect. Both might see it as sealing or establishing the brotherhood or the fellowship of the actors that is felt to be its most fundamental purpose. But it could also be for the actors no more than the sort of festal addition to the specifically efficacious ritual act that Evans-Pritchard claims to have been the case with the Nuer.

To identify the commensality that accompanies a sacrifice as its true purpose is to draw attention to a context and mode of efficacy which the actor, as believer, might well consider to be incidental and not central to the ritual. But this pragmatic mode and context of efficacy, in which it is the function—as a force in the organisation and management of the social and personal relationships of the actors and as a medium for particular cognitive and affective self-realisation—is the context of principal significance for the anthropologist. Agnostic as to the physical reality of the gods or ancestors or other supernatural agencies invoked by the actors, the anthropologist looks to the actors themselves, as individuals and as collectivities, not to the cosmos, as the source of the constructions ('the collective representations') they label gods or ancestors or divinities etc. The ritual is not viewed as a theologian might view it as God-seeking, but rather as in reality serving such purposes as the expression or dramatisation or catharsis, in customary forms, of human cognitive, affective, moral and instrumental, experiences (cf. Beattie 1966). This is the kind of efficacy with which the anthropologist is primarily concerned; and it is consonant with human nature and man's social existence for this efficacy to be achieved sometimes in ways that appear to the observer, no less than to the actor, as realistic and materially appropriate, and at other times in a manner that is best understood as symbolical or non-materially effective. Curing rituals, such as those described and analysed in Victor Turner's studies of Ndembu medicine, illustrate well the procedure. In other words, what is to the theologian a sacrament and to the actor a mystically binding ritual is to the anthropologist *inter alia* a passage rite or a rite of incorporation, often palpably understandable in terms of its manifest form as a communion meal, or a rite of social control.

Thus, whereas the theologian must in the last resort concede that the supernatural agencies and powers, who are deemed by the actors to be the recipients of their sacrifices, stand for really existent supernatural, cosmic, non-terrestrial entities or beings, however dimly cognised, the anthropologist, as Bowker, (*op.cit.* ch.III), demonstrates, must attempt to understand these agencies as conceptualisations or 'objectifications' of otherwise ungraspable and uncontrollable forces of social and individual existence. This is the essence of the Durkheimian hypothesis that society objectifies itself and represents its moral hegemony over individual members in the ceremonies that have their focus in the supernatural agencies towards which devotion and observances are directed. Tylor, earlier, starting from the same premisses of investigation, derived the idea of the supernatural from the doctrine of souls that animate all living things, which he regarded as a logical deduction from such everyday individual experiences as dreaming and from such emotionally-charged dilemmas as how to explain evidence of the apparent continued presence of the dead among the living. In similar vein Malinowski accounted for magic as a symbolic means of coping with anxiety and insecurity in the face of the inevitably uncontrollable and unpredictable factors in every human activity; and Victor Turner sees Ndembu supernatural agencies as projective, symbolical reponses to problems of conflict resolution that arise ultimately from a contradiction between a matrilineal kinship structure and the political and jural supremacy of men. And many other examples could be given, the common principle being to look to human social and psychological proclivities, experiences, and relationships for the sources of the actor's ideas and beliefs about supernatural agencies.

But let me emphasise again that these are all observers' judgements and hypotheses. For the actor, I repeat, his gods, divinities, ancestors, witches, and so forth, are real, if not materially tangible, nevertheless not from his point of view merely symbolical. I recollect how often Tallensi impressed on me that their ancestors were there, present, participating in their own inscrutable way in every sacrifice, even when the offering consisted only of a libation of water, and indeed present in some way during the ordinary affairs of their descendants (cf. Fortes 1977). And I recollect vividly also a high Akan Christian dignitary, a devout and learned leader in his church and community, explaining earnestly to me, one evening after dinner in his house, how he could 'feel' or 'sense' his ancestors near and around him in that room. Among traditional Japanese there is a shrine dedicated to all the family dead, often going back to scores and even hundreds of recorded generations, in the main house of the dispersed family group; and symbolical —because not more than small token—offerings of food and drink are made every day at this shrine, by the housewife, as if they were present there all the time. Similar practices are found, as is well-known, in traditional Chinese lineages (cf. papers by Ooms and Newell in Newell (ed.) 1976).

Thus for peoples like the Tallensi, many other African peoples, the Japanese, the Chinese—and at another level for many pious Christians —the ancestors, gods, saints even the supreme deity are objectively incorporated in the everyday existence of a family or lineage or community at large, in what is to the believer an actually and tangibly accessible form at an altar or shrine. Hayley's paper gives us a beautifully vivid picture of how the deity is brought down and into the group of worshippers, almost, one might conclude, recreated ad hoc each time by his devotees, to receive the offerings made to him. He is then a real presence which the ritual enables the devotees to incorporate, through the food offerings to which he is drawn down, so as to partake with them in the communion of the common meal. It is we, not the devotees, who think that their god is purely imaginary. For them he exists in a way that permits embodiment in comestible offerings and in words and rites that are all materially, tangibly real, efficacious. Regardless of the cultural and geographical distance between them, I am sure that Tallensi, and other West African peoples, would fully understand these rites and relate them to analogous practices in their own religious systems.

As to the symbolic significance of Krishna, this is a complex and many-stranded matter. Hayley suggests that one strand may be reference in it to the model relationship of mother and child. We could speculate that this corresponds to a 'collective representation' or 'objectification' of the sense of dependence and trust and desire of loving care continually reproduced in this 'initial situation' as Malinowski called it, of individual existence; woven into the texture of their social and cultural life, this could well be the basis of the representation his devotees have of Krishna. Thinking along analogous lines I have interpreted some aspects of Tallensi ancestor worship as providing a cultural defence against the disruptive potentialities of the ambivalence that is intrinsic to the relations of successive generations of fathers and sons in patrilineal family systems such as are found among the Tallensi, the Chinese and other peoples (1974). Spiro (1971), Turner (1969) and others have applied variants of such Freudian models in their studies of religious institutions among non-western peoples. What concerns me here, however, is not the particular hypotheses that have emerged in these enquiries, but the implication that their common starting point is the premise that the beliefs and practices they have been concerned with are to be explained in terms of human psychology, social organisation, and cultural resources, not by invoking super-human or extra-human agencies or forces.

Hayley's paper brings me back also to the question as to why objectification in the Durkheimian sense, plays so conspicuous and to all intents universal a part in religious institutions. In the form of material objects like altars, shrines, icons, relics, vestments etc. and in the correlative form of the ritual observances, performances, verbal and non-verbal, of prayer, liturgies, taboos and life-styles, it is clearly fundamental to the practice of sacrifice.

Since from the anthropological point of view Krishna is not really brought down amongst his devotees and Tallensi ancestors are not really present on or in the shrine dedicated to them, the beliefs and practices thus deployed could be described as symbolical. To adapt a well-known saying of Clifford Geertz they could be seen (following Devereux, 1979) as 'symbolical of' cultural representations of filial dependence on parental authority or some other psychological or social constituents of existence in particular human societies or in human society in general. On the other side, from a theological point of view, a great deal of religious belief and ritual is 'symbolical for'—that is to say contains guidance, ideals and sanctions for the conduct of life linked

to doctrines about the terrestrial world, the cosmos, and usually, forms of
continued existence after death. Metaphor, metonym, myths, allegory
and the singularity of a religious 'world of meaning' are invoked to deal
with this. That cautiously sceptical 17th century physician-philosopher,
Sir Thomas Browne, understood the nature of this problem when he
wrote 'for unspeakable mysteries in the Scriptures are often delivered in
a vulgar and illustrative way; and being written unto man are delivered, not as they truly are, but as they may be understood . . .'
(*Religio Medici*, p.52).

The postscript to our symposium by Barrington-Ward and Bourdillon
is concerned with this issue, when, for instance, they say that 'in
coming together for a sacrificial rite, people express acceptance of the
principal cosmological symbols and of the moral ideals which the
prescribed ritual contains'. The sacrifice of Christ, they say, has for
Christians 'universal application yet remains a concrete symbol', a
peculiar reality even though understood metaphorically. The Mass
thus appears as a symbolic ritual in relation to which a world view and a
scheme of moral conduct are appropriated by each actor.

Granted then, that for the believer, ritual, and in the present instance
specifically the ritual of a sacrificial offering, is deemed to be efficacious
(failure being accountable for within the framework of the supporting
beliefs, as many authorities from Tylor onward have explained) can
general principles—relating, for example, to the believed efficacy of
sacrifice—be discerned? Both Beattie and Bourdillon appear to doubt
the possibility of this, considering the great diversity and flexibility,
material, situational, and symbolical of sacrifice in different cultures.
The various theories they review—gift theory, communion theory,
abnegation theory, power mobilising theory etc.—all appear to have
only limited validity. Of more general application is the Maussian
formula for what Evans-Pritchard called the 'grammar' of sacrifice
(1964, viii), with its focus on the act of consecration and its climax in
the act of immolation. But this tells us nothing about the function or the
meaning of sacrifice either for the actor or for the observer.

One feature is clear enough. It is a special ritual procedure for
establishing or mobilising a relationship of mutuality between the
donor (individual or collective) and the recipient; and there is generally,
if not always, an implication of mutual constraint, and indeed of actual
or potential mutual coercion in the act. This is a feature of sacrifice in
practice that immediately impresses a participant ethnographer in the
field. Sacrifice is more commonly a response to a demand or command
from supernatural agencies or else a rendering of a standard obligation,
than a spontaneous offering; and whether or not it is thought of as

persuasion for act

expiation or propitiation or purgation, there is commonly an element of demand, certainly of persuasion, on the donor's side.

Most commonly, as I suggested earlier, the relationship established or mobilised is one of dependence on the donor's side quite palpably modelled on, and a transformation of, the submissive filial dependence ideally expected of offspring in relation to parents. This is a form of dependence in which a sense of impotence and vulnerability is engendered by reason of the inevitable and necessary parental control and care. This sense of impotence and vulnerability is, I believe, deeply ingrained in human consciousness, being continually reinforced by the experience of pain, suffering, and deprivation. And it is a fact of human existence that in all societies receives elaborate customary expression. Founded, as I am suggesting, in the universal infantile experience of helpless dependency, it is continually substantiated and, so to say, objectively validated by experience of environmental hazards, social crises and other such external pressures.

From this angle, sacrifice falls into a wider class of what might be called rituals of defence. It is noteworthy how often the demands for sacrifice on the part of a supernatural agency are signalled by affliction or misfortune, interpreted by the worshippers as punishment for sin or its equivalent, or as warning of troubles to come. Even the joyous sacrifices associated with passage rites, with calendrical (i.e. sowing or harvest) festivals, or in commemoration of historical or mythological events, have an obvious prophylactic intention. Whether the ostensible intention is to get rid of or drive away the supernatural agency believed to be the source of the affliction (as Evans-Pritchard, taking a cue from Old Testament sacrifice, interprets Nuer sacrifice to aim at); or, conversely, to enlist the good will of the dangerous supernatural agencies by incorporating them into the communion of the family or the congregation of worshippers, as is the case among peoples like the Tallensi and the Assamese devotees; the common aim is to defend the donors. And it is defence against what I have described as the inescapable vulnerability of humanity, vulnerability to the unexpected, unpredictable and uncontrollable fact of disease or hunger or war or social upheaval that appear to come upon us from the outside, or alternatively the internal vulnerability to the weakness of body or mind which become manifest as lust or anger, jealousy or hate, as sin or mental disorder, and ultimately of course to the totally inescapable vulnerability to death and annihilation.[2] Even sacrifices defined as thanks offerings have a defensive aspect since they purport to be given in gratitude for recovery from affliction or for good fortune or survival, and more often in the spirit of repaying a debt rather than as an expression of spontaneous love.

Although as Rogerson points out, we have only texts that formulate rules and regulations of sacrifice, and no ethnographic data on the actual conduct of the rites, the Old Testament patterns of sacrifice he discusses are most instructive in this connection. It is interesting to see how many forms of sacrifice are prescribed by divine law to expiate unwitting— that, is, unconsciously motivated rather than intentional—wrong-doing. These are sacrifices for the removal of pollution, whether for such natural occurrences as birth and death, or for leprosy which falls into the same class as pollution, being of course passively, that is not intentionally, incurred. ·And this is equally true for the calendrically fixed festivals.

The defensive character of Old Testament sacrifice is apparent all through. And likewise, there is generally an implication of sacrifice being obligatory as if in payment of a debt, neglect of which could be disastrous. Most of all, the rules of Old Testament sacrifice testify to the mutually coercive relationship of God, on his part insisting on unquestioning obedience to his laws and his unique authority, and the Hebrews, on their part, appealing, often in tones that sound demanding rather than ingratiating, for his fatherly support and protection in spite of their lapses from perfect filial submission; and all this on the strength of the reciprocal commitments implied in the original Covenant. This pattern fits in with the compromise institution of the Temple- and priest-centred cult which, on the one hand, insulates the worshippers from direct contact with and exposure to the dangerous holiness of God, and on the other, purports by means of the sacrifice to bring him into the temple, and thus make him subject to intercession on behalf of the community in the name of the moral norms of kinship amity, as Robertson-Smith conjectured. It is significant that the generic concept for sacrifice in the Old Testament (and in Arabic) is *korban*, as Rogerson notes, from a root meaning to bring near, as if to express a yearning which could never be satisfied. Typically, moreover, as is the case in many other societies, Old Testament sacrifice was never spontaneous, but as Rogerson says 'it was enough that God commanded the sacrifice and Israel should obey the commands'. Hence perhaps the emphasis on sacrifice as expiation of or atonement for unwitting sin or ritual defilement.

In every case—whether the aim of sacrifice as the actor sees it is to thrust away, or, alternatively, to bring near and incorporate—the first step must always be to bring the supernatural power down from his or its sacred world or its hidden existence into the everyday human world where people talk to one another, argue out their disputes and express their emotion in the open. A sacrifice very dramatically brings

into the open of an assembly of worshippers entitled and qualified by
kinship or descent, or other criteria of membership of the congregation, the circumstances to which it is the proper customary response.
This is of necessity a ritual response, since by definition it is impossible
for transactions with supernatural powers to be undertaken by secular
means. And it makes sense that the ritual of bringing the occult agency
'down to earth' so to speak, to become accessible at an altar for instance,
should require the mediation of a material offering. Furthermore an
offering that lends itself to presentation in terms of the basic vehicle of
kinship mutuality, that is to say the shared meal, would seem to be
particularly apt. Its cardinal significance in Old Testament sacrifice
was emphasised not only by Robertson-Smith but by other semiticists
of his generation, as Rogerson points out. God is thought of as sharing
the sacrificial meal in a quite concrete way. The burning of choice
parts or even of the whole of the victim is seen as providing 'a sweet
savour unto the Lord'.[3]

The theme of blood sacrifice and other offerings being intended by
the actor to be in a ritual sense, even to some extent in a material
sense, food for the supernatural recipient, is so prominent everywhere
that it is surprising to find it overlooked in some theoretical discussions,
though Robertson-Smith of course gave it high priority. Starting from
the model of sacrifice being normatively an offering from a filial
dependant to a parental divinity, the feeding theme can be seen as
implying a reversal, in the ritual context, of the food dependency relationship in the context of living reality. It is almost as if the dependent
worshipper is by this means enabled to redefine himself as the dominant
quasi-parental sustainer of the divinity's existence, and therefore entitled to make demands on him.

Eating and drinking of sanctified offerings is not only the model for,
but is seen by the actor as, the efficacious means of incorporating the
divinity into both the commensal group and the consciousness of each of
its members. This is what makes it so fundamental a feature in the ritual
of sacrifice (cf. Harris, 1978). It signifies the transformation of what is at
first responded to as a punitive or rejecting, usually remote supernatural agency, into a good, protective, close at hand mystical presence.
And to understand better why incorporation of divinity through the
symbolism of the shared meal is so potent, one must think also of its
contrary, namely fasting, and other forms of abstinence, as sacrificial
practices. Whatever else such forms of self-mortification may signify,
their self-defensive character is patent.

The Hebraic notion, taken over by both theologians and some
anthropologists, that the life is in the blood and that it is this life that is

the essential offering in a blood sacrifice, looks like God's law of talion in reverse, and this does perhaps make plausible some form of 'ransom' explanation of Hebrew and Nuer types of sacrifice. It is relevant however to bear in mind what Hubert and Mauss particularly emphasised; the only way living humans can be sure of establishing reciprocal communication with the supernatural agencies on the other side of the mystical curtain separating the profane from the sacred world, is through a mediator that is qualified by sacrificial death or its equivalent (for e.g. vegetable offerings). This is, from the actor's point of view, the essential condition for entry into the 'other world' whether the eventual aim is to ensure that the supernatural agencies depart and stop intervening in the 'profane' human world, or whether it is to bring them nearer and into that world.

My aim, here, has not been to propose alternatives to current anthropological theories of sacrifice. It has been to illustrate ways in which an anthropological approach is likely to differ from a theological approach to the study of sacrifice. Concluding his discussion on Old Testament sacrifice, Rogerson sums up the differences neatly as follows: 'the latter [i.e. the anthropologist] would presumably concentrate upon the structure and function of the sacrifice. The theologian would concentrate upon sacrifice as seen in terms of the story, and the insight into eternal reality which that story might contain'. In the more prosaic language of anthropology that 'eternal reality' might perhaps be glossed as signifying universal moral values and realisation of the ultimate inscrutability of Nature and of the human situation.

But if the differences between a theological point of view and an anthropological point of view in the study of sacrifice and other religious institutions is obvious, I think it is fair to add that our symposium gives plenty of evidence of common interests and overlapping procedures of enquiry. There is great promise here of the further collaboration which Tylor called for over a century ago.

NOTES

1. From the actor's point of view, as I argue later in this paper, sacrifice must, like any other ritual, be deemed to be efficacious, that is, it must be deemed to fulfil the manifest purpose of the ritual act. This does not mean that it is expected to be successful in every case. For as has long been emphasised every religious system (like every therapeutic system, scientific no less than magical, and many technical systems) provides rationalisations and loopholes for the explanation of the failure of

particular ritual acts. But, as Tylor, Frazer, Durkheim et al. and many later writers have pointed out, failure in an individual case does not destroy the belief in the efficacy of ritual from the actor's point of view. It is around this problem of efficacy that much of the theoretical debate over the meaning and function of ritual revolves. For as I note above, the efficacy of ritual as the anthropologist sees it is of a different order from that of the actor. Hence we find anthropologists having recourse to Austinian notions about 'performative' or 'illocutionary' utterances. The problem of efficacy as it appears from the opposed interests of actor-believer and observer-anthropologist are cogently analysed in Ahern's paper in *Man* (1979).

2. We may think ourselves exempt from this, but enormously as the threshold of vulnerability has been raised by advances in science, technology, medicine and social organisation in our society, the sense of vulnerability still remains with us—in matters of health, economic and social well being, personal and collective existence etc. Does it not lie behind the whole range of compensating values and practices reflected in our political ideologies and in our moral norms? Does it not play a large part in the proliferation of escapist and salvationist cults, not infrequently of oriental origin, throughout the Western world? Environmental and world-political hazards of an apparently arbitrary kind, unpredictability of the course of personal and social life, and the inevitabilities of disease and death, continue to haunt us and to evoke social and psychological defence reactions which are as apt to take religious or magical forms as among pre-scientific peoples.

3. It is interesting to reflect how widespread is the belief that impulses and motives which are secret or repressed, by cultural definition, are the sources of practices magically or mystically dangerous to others, as in witchcraft and sorcery or the 'anger of the heart' recently described by Grace Harris (1978). In contrast, as she explains, the same impulses and motives openly admitted are likely to be regarded as evidence of human frailty which may cause conflict and trouble, but of an open kind that can be resolved by legal or religious measures or simply in open discussion. It is a principle that has general validity as most psycho-therapists would agree.

REFERENCES

Ahern, Emily M. 1979. 'The Problem of efficacy; strong and weak illocutionary acts', *Man* (n.s.) 14 (1), 1–18.

Beattie, J. 1966. 'Ritual and Social Change', *Man* (n.s.), 1 (1), 60–74.

Bowker, John. 1973. *The Sense of God*. Oxford: Clarendon Press.

Browne, Sir Thomas. 1643. *Religio Medici*. Reprinted in 1968. *Selected Writings*, (ed.) Geoffrey Keynes. London: Faber.

Devereux, George 1979. Fantasy and Symbol as Dimensions of Reality.' In *Fantasy and Symbol: Studies in Anthropological Interpretation* (ed.) R. H. Hook. London: Academic Press.

Evans-Pritchard, E. E. 1937. *Witchcraft, Oracles and Magic among the Azande.* Oxford: Clarendon Press.

────── 1950. 'Social Anthropology; Past and Present', The Marett Lecture, *Man*, 50.

────── 1956. *Nuer Religion.* Oxford: Clarendon Press.

────── 1964. Foreword to English translation of Henri Hubert and Marcel Mauss *Essai sur la Nature et la Fonction du Sacrifice*, Ann. Sociologique vol. II, 1899. London: Cohen and West.

Fortes, Meyer 1966. 'Religious premises and logical technique in Divinatory ritual' in 'A Discussion on Ritualization of behaviour in animals and man'. Organised by Sir Julian Huxley, F.R.S. *Phil. Trans. Royal Society*, Series B., no. 772, vol. 251, 410–422.

────── 1974. 'The First Born.' *J. Child Psychol. Psychiat.* 15, 81–104.

────── 1977. 'Custom and Conscience in Anthropological Perspective.' *Int. Rev. Psycho-anal.* 4, 127–154.

Harris G. G. 1978. *Casting out anger: religion among the Taita of Kenya.* Cambridge: University Press.

Horton, Robin and Finnegan, Ruth (eds.) 1973. *Modes of Thought; Essays on Thinking in Western and non-Western Societies.* London: Faber.

Newell, W. H. (ed.) 1976. *Ancestors.* The Hague: Mouton.

Otto, Rudolf 1917. *Das Heilige.* English translation by J. W. Harvey, second edition 1950, *The Idea of the Holy.* London: Oxford University Press.

Spiro, M. 1971. *Buddhism and Society; A Great Tradition and its Burmese vicissitudes.* London: Allen and Unwin.

Turner, Victor W. 1969. *The Ritual Process.* Chicago: Aldine Press.

Tylor, E. B. 1871. *Primitive Culture.* Fifth edition, 1929, 2 volumes. London: John Murray.

Wilson, Monica 1951. *Good Company: A Study of Nyakyusa Age Villages.* London: Oxford University Press.

────── 1956. *Rituals of Kinship among the Nyakyusa.* London: Oxford University Press.

────── 1971. *Religion and the Transformation of Society.* Cambridge: University Press.

ACKNOWLEDGEMENTS

Acknowledgements are due first to Jonathan Benthall, director of the Royal Anthropological Institute, who was the principal convenor of the conference on sacrifice, and who has contributed much time and attention to the mechanics of having this collection of papers published. Also to Simon Barrington-Ward, co-convenor of the conference; Cornelius Ernst, O.P., for ideas in the planning stage; the principal, Walter James, the staff of Cumberland Lodge and the Trustees of St. Catharine's, for providing such agreeable accommodation for the conference; the Social Science Research Council French Programme for a grant towards the cost of having a French contribution to the conference; the University of Calabar for enabling the principal editor of this volume to attend; to all who participated in the conference, whether by formal presentation of papers or by discussion at formal and informal sessions, for providing stimulus to develop and to clarify the thoughts presented in this volume; and to Patricia Peach for secretarial assistance.

M.F.C.B.

CONTENTS

INTRODUCTION

M. F. C. Bourdillon

This collection of essays arose from a meeting between social anthropologists and Christian theologians under the auspices of the Royal Anthropological Institute and St Catharine's Foundation at Cumberland Lodge, Windsor Great Park in February 1979. Both groups of scholars have a long tradition of interest in the subject of sacrifice: anthropologists because of the central place sacrifice has in so many cultures throughout the world, and theologians because sacrifice is a central feature of the Judaeo-Christian understanding of man's relationship with God. Yet sacrifice, in its common form of ritual slaughter, has little place in the cultures of modern, technologically developed societies. How are we to make sense of this widespread phenomenon? Does it have anything to say to us today?

This volume presents the main ideas which came out of the conference. Unfortunately, for various reasons we were not able to include all the papers presented at the conference. There are two papers which indicate the anthropological approaches to the subject, those by Dr Beattie and Dr Hayley; and two studies of the Judaeo-Christian tradition by theologians, namely Professor Rogerson and Professor Sykes. To these are added an anthropological study of contemporary Christian sacrifice by Dr Campbell-Jones, and a postscript, theological in emphasis, on the present status of the symbol of sacrifice. But as we shall see, there is no simple separation of anthropology and theology.

I. THE APPROACHES OF ANTHROPOLOGISTS AND THEOLOGIANS

Anthropologists and theologians start their investigations into sacrifice in much the same way. Both disciplines begin by looking at animal sacrifices in the history of religions, and analyse the meanings of these rites in their various cultural contexts.

Theologians start with the sacrifices of the ancient Hebrews recorded in the Old Testament, and seek clues to their understanding
from comparisons with sacrifices in other societies of the ancient near
east. Theologians may also look for insight from sacrifices of comparable
contemporary societies, for which they consult the studies of anthropologists, and the general theories about sacrifice that have come from
them. Rogerson warns us of how sketchy is available knowledge on
the ancient Hebrews. Nevertheless, since the Christian understanding
of the world grew out of this ancient religion, our starting-point for a
theological understanding of Christian sacrifice must be an analysis
of whatever data we have on the meaning of the sacrifices of the
ancient Hebrews to the people who performed them.

Anthropologists pay more attention to the sacrifices of people who
still perform them. Anthropological researchers are able to observe
these sacrifices at first hand, and so to examine their place in the lives
and thought of the participants. They can collect information relevant
to their own interests, and are not hampered by enormous gaps resulting
from the very different interests of ancient chroniclers. Like theologians,
anthropologists are aided in their analyses by what other scholars have
said about sacrifices among other peoples; indeed, such comparison,
which leads to general principles rather than to the detailed knowledge
of a particular culture, is a central feature of social anthropology.

The methodological overlap between anthropology and theology is
illustrated by Rogerson's list of anthropological ideas useful to theologians who are trying to interpret Old Testament sacrifices. When he
points out the importance to theologians of the narrative recited in
conjunction with the Passover 'sacrifice', he is in accord with, for example, studies of Dogon sacrifice by French anthropologists, who
analyse the rites with reference to a primal myth about creation and
order which is symbolized and re-enacted in sacrificial ritual (cf.
Dieterlen 1976; de Heusch 1976b). Dieterlen's study of Dogon symbols
shows the links between Dogon sacrifices, their myths and the way they
structure their social life; Sykes's study of the implications of Christian
symbols shows the links between Christian sacrifice, the basic Christian
story, and Christian ideals for a moral life. The difference between
anthropology and theology lies not so much in their respective theoretical methods of analysis, as in the evaluation of the communication
which analytical interpretation reveals.

There is, however, a dimension which social anthropology clearly
adds to the kind of interpretation of symbols offered in common by
anthropologists and theologians. Anthropologists relate what people
say or believe to the patterns of social relationships in which they live.

In this volume, Campbell-Jones links three types of interpretation of the Mass to three different patterns of convent life, in a study which is clearly different from any theological analysis. She is concerned not so much with a systematic search for a coherent meaning to the symbols the nuns use, as with explaining the interpretations of the nuns in terms of their social relations, and particularly of their hierarchical structures. Hayley also illustrates this approach of social anthropology in, for example, her appeal to marriage customs in the interpretation of religious offerings—an appeal which will find parallels in theological studies. Hayley warns, however, against too ready an assumption that ritual can be explained in terms of social structure: she argues that ideas of caste and rank, so dominant in Hindu social life, are foreign to the spirit of the religious offerings she describes. The social dimension is usually significant in the explanations of why people use particular symbols and perform particular rites, but it does not always help in the interpretation of what people mean by their symbols—what they understand and what they intend to achieve. Although theologians do not, and should not, entirely ignore social explanations, anthropologists place more emphasis on such factors. This leads us to a fundamental difference between the two disciplines.

Notwithstanding many shared points in methodology, anthropology and theology differ in their aims. The aim of social anthropologists with respect to sacrifice could be summarized as an examination of sacrifices in a variety of social and cultural contexts, in order to learn more about the nature of man in society. A Christian theologian looks for any truth communicated by the sacrifices he studies: he tries to build up from the Judaeo-Christian tradition a concept of sacrifice which can be used meaningfully in contemporary situations. This aim involves an evaluative, as well as an analytic, element in the examination of sacrifices in history: theology tries to discern what aspects of these sacrifices can meaningfully be preserved and incorporated into contemporary symbolic expression. There are, therefore, two points in this contrast in aims: they concern the place of doctrine and the place of value-judgements.

In drawing this simplified contrast, I do not wish to obscure the complexity and variety of aims to be found within each of the disciplines. Theologians vary in their emphases and aims from a descriptive, phenomenological study of Christian religion (and perhaps of religion in general) on the one hand, to the exposition of dogma and consequent exhortation on the other. On the part of anthropologists, their exposition of the meaning of religious symbols and the value-judgements they make can bring their discipline close to certain approaches within theology.

Taking first the question of value-judgements, it has been argued that anthropology aims to be value-free. When an anthropologist studies the moral values of a culture or society, his aim is to try to understand them independently of the values of his own or any other culture. Although no one can be completely free of value-judgements, most anthropologists aim to keep their studies free of prejudices which pretend to determine how people should behave. It is, on the other hand, extremely rare to find a Christian theologian who does not hold that his discipline is concerned with ideals for living.

Yet the history of social anthropology reveals strong links with the sphere of moral judgements. Emile Durkheim believed that his new science of society would involve an evaluation of established moral opinion, and provide a guide to moral choice (cf. Lukes 1975: 425—8). It is a common view among anthropologists that their discipline does challenge established morals, and that the study of moral ideas in a variety of cultures is a relevant corrective to certain ethical theories. The modern radical movement in anthropology takes this principle a step further: radicals argue that the discipline leads to particular social ethics. The discipline often embodies an hortatory element, not very different from the indirect way in which most academic theology relates to normative behaviour.[1]

As for doctrine, certainly anthropologists do not claim that their discipline can pronounce on the nature of any deity that some may believe to exist. But many theologians would also balk at such a task. Rather they regard their task as to analyse and adjust the symbolic system of their tradition in order to probe problem areas and to remove inconsistencies, both inconsistencies internal to the system and inconsistencies between the system as it has been received and contemporary experience. Doctrinal speculation involves the interpretation of symbols from past experience into language that is more immediately in touch with contemporary experience and which is logically consistent.[2] Sykes's analysis in this collection is concerned with the basic problem of incorporating the symbols of sacrifice into a Christian world of meaning. This is partly an historical problem (and on the historical side Hayward's appendix links the Old and the New Testaments). But it is also something more: the theologian's analysis of the symbol of sacrifice attempts to communicate something cognitive and moral about human life.

Parallels to theological interpretation can be found in anthropology. The impetus was provided by Evans-Pritchard's analysis of Nuer religious symbolism (1956). A more explicit example is V. W. Turner's study of the ritual symbols of the Ndembu people of Zambia. Here the anthropologist deliberately takes his analysis of meaning beyond what the Ndembu themselves recognise (1967: 26)—his initial exegesis was in any case worked out in conversations with a Ndembu ritual specialist, whom Turner considered to be the equivalent of a philosophy don (1967: ch.6)—and relates Ndembu symbols to fundamental symbols in his own culture (1962: 82—96). In such work, he is taking on the role of Ndembu philosopher or theologian. In discussion at the conference on sacrifice, the French anthropologist Michel Cartry explained his analysis of sacrifice among the Gourmantche of the Upper Volta (cf. Cartry 1976) by saying that he saw one of the tasks of anthropology as to re-create incomplete myths in order to make more systematic the symbols and explanations which are explicitly understood and cited by the people who use them. This surely is very close to the theologian's task of systematizing the thought and experience of Christian people.

Where theology is clearly different from anthropology is in the former's specific focus on the symbols of a particular living tradition, and their interpretation. Theology studies the traditions from within, and consequently maintains the right to criticise the tradition as received and to instigate change within it. Anthropologists look at different cultures from the point of view of outsiders: their task is to understand the traditions they study, and to criticise only the ideas they receive from their own culture. They are not normally in a position to try to reform the traditions they study.

Stephen Sykes's argument, that the death of Jesus as portrayed by New Testament writers is a real sacrifice, implies a judgement that the symbol of sacrifice should not be dropped by the Christian body. R. J. Daly (1978) examines the history of sacrifice in Judaism and Christianity, showing how the emphasis moved from ritual performances of ancient Judaism to the internal dispositions of early Christians and their practical works of service: Daly claims that this is relevant to a 'proper understanding of Christianity itself' (p.135), and clearly his argument affects Christian norms of behaviour. Frances Young concludes her theological analysis of Christian sacrifice (1975) with a chapter which suggests how the symbol can carry meaning in a contemporary western world, pointing to psychological needs in man and powerful related symbols in literature. Theologians not only analyse symbols in their historical and social contexts, but also suggest to the reader ways of thinking about fundamental issues.

Anthropologists cannot prescribe in this way. Possibly attempts like that of Young to relate sacrifice to life in the contemporary humanistic world would gain for anthropologists greater sensitivity to the sacrifices they study.

This leads to a question that arises in theological rather than anthropological thought, namely, that of 'efficacy'. What are the conditions under which sacrifice can achieve its desired or intended effects?

The early humanist anthropologists dismissed the rites of religion as based on logical error, and presumed that the rites were simply not efficacious. Sir Edward Tylor's explicit aim in his exploration of social evolution was to expose the false basis of all theology. Later anthropologists turned their attention to the effects of rituals on other aspects of social life; they speculated on how rites help to maintain social values (A. R. Radcliffe-Brown 1922), how ritual provides psychological security in dangerous situations (B. Malinowski 1948), how it supports the structure of and order in a society (Emile Durkheim 1915), how rites control the way participants experience the world and its events (R. G. Lienhardt 1961), and so on. In this kind of analysis, the reasons that participants give for religious actions have at best secondary importance. When contemporary anthropologists returned to the hermeneutic interpretation of ritual, their concern was to explicate a coherent system of symbolic thought, within which rituals can be understood as expressive drama. On the relationship between the effects of rituals and what participants expect to achieve through them, anthropologists have on the whole retained an embarrassed silence.[3]

For theologians, however, this relationship is crucial. Theologians are part of the tradition they study, and must be convinced that their rituals have the effects that they want them to have. What different members of the Christian tradition want and expect from their rituals varies enormously, and reflects a wide variety of cosmologies. Some are concerned primarily with 'other worldly' effects on souls and an after life. Others are concerned with reinforcing a world of meaning which is not only coherent in itself but also consistent with events in the material world. Others, again, look for social and pragmatic effects, very similar to—if not identical with—the functions of rites which anthropologists readily accept.[4] Whatever the world view of a particular theologian, he is concerned with what he believes to be the real effects of the rituals of his tradition, and consequently with what is necessary to make such rituals efficacious. Sykes's analysis makes it clear that the efficacy of Christian sacrifice arises from the lives of the persons making the offering.

Even here there is room for dialogue. A recent anthropological study of the traditional religion of the Taita of Kenya (Harris 1978) deals explicitly with the question of efficacy. The author analyses the social pre-conditions that the Taita themselves demand if their rites are to be successful in casting out dangerous anger from the community, and the sickness they believe to be consequent on such anger. She relates these criteria to conditions an outsider might see as necessary for overcoming social tension. When performers and anthropological observers can agree about the real effects of symbolic action—in matters concerning health, for example, or the social order—the value to anthropologists of the performers' ideas of the efficacy of rites is clear. To probe into how they understand the efficacy of other rituals can be equally enlightening.

This leads us to the question of the distinction between magic and religion, a distinction which has proved so problematic in anthropology, but which provides little difficulty for theologians. The common English concept of 'magic' derives from attempts to manipulate events through esoteric knowledge of spirits or of material substances, attempts which have been superseded in European history by empirical science. 'Magic' has become an ethnocentric, value-laden term, referring to attempts to control events by means which the speaker does not believe in.

This usage was the basis of early evolutionary theories of magic, like those of Sir James Frazer and E. B. Tylor (who considered magic and religion to be equally illusory); but it was unacceptable to later anthropologists who were concerned to overcome ethnocentric prejudices against the peoples they studied. It has not, however, been easy to replace such usage with a satisfactory definition of magic in social terms which do not presuppose the cultural superiority of the anthropological observer.

Durkheim (1915: 43—5) defined a distinction between magic and religion in terms of the private nature of the former and the public nature of the latter. For him, religion is always related to some kind of group or community, whose unity it serves to maintain. Durkheim pointed out that magic is often the antithesis of religion and hostile to sacred things: it is operated for individual aims, independently of the needs or controls of the community in which it is practised.

This distinction is not without difficulty. There are private activities, particularly those associated with mysticism, which are usually classified as religious. Durkheim argues that such private cults are elemental aspects of the community as a whole; but the same could be argued for many 'magical' rites. On the other hand, there are public rituals, such as rain-making, which have much in common with magical activities in the sense that their primary purpose is to produce some material effect. Whether it is a group or an individual who aims to benefit is not relevant to the cognitive process implied in a common

understanding of the word 'magic'. Durkheim's distinction points to
social characteristics which are often to be found in magic and religion
respectively, but it is not satisfactory for the purpose of defining the
two terms.

E. R. Leach (1964) followed a common use of the term 'magic'
when he defined it as attempts by individuals or groups to control
their environment, using means which are untested, and often untest-
able, by the methods of empirical science. According to this definition
magic is distinguished from science since the former rests on untested
belief, and from religion since magic is an attempt at control. Against
such a distinction, R. G. Lienhardt (1961: 245, 283) pointed out that
Dinka religious rituals were often attempts at control, and that apparently magical acts should not be mistaken for primitive technology.
Like religious rituals, they are expressive of wishes and intentions, and
do not replace direct action to achieve one's ends when such action
is possible. Although Lienhardt was speaking specifically of the Dinka
of the Southern Sudan, his observations can be applied widely, and
Beattie's contribution points out the expressive nature of 'magical'
rites generally.

In a later work (1976: 29—32), Leach argues that the logic of magic
is based on the failure to distinguish signs and symbols from causative
signals; and he points out that technical actions performed habitually
can become very similar to magic. This is an important observation, as
it draws attention away from particular actions, and turns instead to
the attitudes and intentions of the person performing the action. An
expressive action, or a technical action, can become magical through a
failure (perhaps due to habit) to reflect on the precise nature of the
action. Understood in this way, 'magic' keeps something of its deroga-
tory connotation; but cannot be readily applied to any particular class
of action, still less to a particular culture.

For anthropologists, the difficulty has been to redefine a term with
strong ethnocentric connotations for use in a discipline which assumes
cultural relativity: this difficulty does not arise for theologians, whose
discipline is culturally specific. A theologian has no difficulty in using
'magic' to refer to rituals which others, and not he, believe to be efficacious. In particular, he can describe as 'magical', attitudes to rituals
within his own tradition which he believes should be rejected. In
religious circles, rituals are often referred to as magical when the persons
performing them believe that they automatically receive some kind of
benefit from the rituals, without paying sufficient attention to conditions
necessary for their efficacy. In this sense, we are not so much distinguishing magical from religious rites, as magical elements or attitudes in the

way religious rites are performed. Anthropologists and theologians might well agree on a definition of magic in these terms, especially when a theologian demands from rituals an empirical effect in the lives and social relations of the persons performing them.[5] Yet such a usage still implies that what is discerned to be magical should ideally be discarded; and anthropologists, as outsiders, are rightly diffident about telling people what of their ritual tradition they should keep and what they should reject. A theologian, who is within the tradition he is studying, feels no such inhibition.

What is true from the points of view of both anthropology and theology is that we should be very cautious about labelling any particular action as 'magic'. Among the participants performing any particular ritual, there are likely to be degrees of sophistication in the ways they understand their actions. At least some in any group are likely to recognise the symbolic and expressive nature of rituals which superficially appear to be manipulative in intention. The studies of sacrifice in this volume attempt to explicate the symbolism and the rationale of various sacrifices, on the presumption that none can simply be dismissed as magic and irrelevant to the modern world.

A further idea that Leach expounds in his analysis of the logic of sacrifice (1976: 81—93) is that sacred rituals are performed in an ambiguous, liminal area, mediating between 'This World of temporal experience' (A) and 'The Other World of experience-reversed' (not A—Leach does not explain why people concern themselves with this non-world). According to a second model, ritual (in this case sacrifice) makes ordinary time appear discontinuous by inserting periods of 'sacred non-time' into the ordinary flow of secular time.

Something of what Leach says is true. Ritual often seeks to maintain contact between ordinary life and what is in some sense sacred (though not necessarily Other-Worldly); and ritual does sometimes insulate a particular action from precepts and values which are operative in ordinary life (an idea I shall be using). The structuralist approach, however, that identifies the 'Other World' mediated by sacred ritual with 'experience-reversed', is to my mind a gross oversimplification. The world communicated in religious ritual may be a number of things: often it incorporates an ideal, found only imperfectly in real life; it may be a millenarian dream, incorporating all good things from this world and no bad things; it may consist of personified influences, in terms of spirits of the dead and other spiritual powers; it may express an attempt to cope with the more profound problems of life; it may incorporate many other themes. In all of these some difference from what pertains in ordinary life is implied, and often emphasized; but some continuity and similarity with ordinary life is also implied. To focus, as Leach does, on the differences and to ignore the continuities is to distort the place of the 'sacred' in the cognitive lives of those who use it, and consequently to distort the cognitive functions of ritual.

A more serious and related theory is that ritual does communicate ideas about this world, but that these ideas conceal or distort the real nature of things, especially in favour of traditional authority.[6] Certainly people sometimes have distorted ideas of reality, and these can be expressed in ritual as in many other ways. Ritual can also be used by people in authority to distort the truth in order to exploit their subjects more efficiently. Sometimes, however, ritual expresses more realistic views. Thus V. W. Turner, in an analysis of certain Ndembu sacrifices, argues against Claude Lévi-Strauss that far from hiding discrepancies between Ndembu society and their ideals, the rites arise out of an awareness of such discrepancies in social antagonism, and attempt to restore society to an ideal state of 'communitas' (1977: esp 196): Turner argues that, unlike the state-controlled Iguvian sacrifices, in the African case symbolic death in sacrifice expresses a sensitivity to changing social relations (1977: 208—9). In this volume, Sykes's analysis is an attempt to communicate through the symbols of Christian sacrifice something real and profound about life in this world.

II.   THE SCOPE OF THE STUDY

There are three meanings of the word 'sacrifice' in common English usage. The slaughter of an animal or person, or the surrender of a possession, in ritual; the destruction or surrender of something for the sake of something else, normally of higher value; and the Mass. None of these corresponds exactly with the etymological meaning, making sacred, which however, as Beattie explains, describes an important characteristic of many ritual sacrifices. The word can be, and has been, applied to a wide variety of human actions, not all of which are the concern of the present studies.

The essays in this collection are concerned with religious ritual sacrifices, that is, sacrificial rites which in some way are central to the lives of the people who perform them, expressing and communicating fundamental beliefs and values. Such sacrifices communicate a world of meaning (to use Sykes's phrase). To explain this focus, I shall draw attention to, and comment upon, a number of types of sacrifice with which the authors are not primarily concerned—although they may highlight themes which are important in the more central religious sacrifices.

Calculated Sacrifices

One denotation of sacrifice (which Sykes calls sacrifice only by metaphor) applies to various areas of human activity, such as politics or business transactions or a game of chess, when something of value is surrendered in the expectation or hope of greater gain. Sacrifice in this sense is a calculated action, normally involving a weighing of alternative material advantages. Such a sacrifice does not necessarily involve a cultural pool of symbols, and is not normally concerned with ultimate cosmologies or a world of meaning, features which are central to the religious sacrifices with which these studies are primarily concerned.

Some anthropologists have argued that even ritual sacrifices should be understood in terms of material gains expected from them. Marvin Harris (1978: 99—110), for example, argues that Aztec human sacrifices are a response by ruling classes to a shortage of protein in the ecology, a thesis which at best is highly speculative.[7] More seriously, Raymond Firth (1963) has discussed the economics of ritual sacrifice, conceived as an offering by man of resources which could have some other use: to some extent this involves a rational calculation of the cost of resources against expected benefits to be received from the supernatural powers to whom they are offered, be these benefits of a specific or a generalized nature. Firth points out the importance of community values in controlling what can legitimately be given up in order to obtain supernatural favours, a point we shall be returning to later.

Another writer who has emphasized economic factors in sacrifice, though from a different point of view, is O. Herrenschmidt (1978). He argues that one of the first questions to ask is who pays for the sacrifice, since this will indicate the '*sacrifiant*', the person (or group) on whose behalf the sacrifice is offered. In his discussion of Hindu sacrifices, Herrenschmidt points out that the person who pays hopes to benefit from the sacrifice; he chooses the religious experts to perform it (they are mere technicians), and the nature of the object to be sacrificed; his desire or intention is necessary for the efficacy of the sacrifice. The object of sacrifice is not the gods, but the benefit to be derived from them; and the benefit is derived by means of an action which usually has a forbidden air about it, a symbolic crime. These observations are particularly apt for those sacrifices which feature magical and sorcerous characteristics; and more generally, Herrenschmidt is right to warn us against giving all our attention to the cosmology and ritual symbolism of religious experts, to the exclusion of the laity—who to some extent control the rituals.

Certainly, an economic element often comes into religious sacrifices.

Since a religious world of meaning is normally associated with concomitant social values, we can expect religious rituals which communicate the world of meaning to include something of the economic relations of society. When significant economic cost is incurred, an analysis of the sacrifice must take note of who pays the cost and who expects to profit from the action. A calculation of material gain may be an element in religious sacrifice, but it is not always present.[8] Particularly when sacrifice is a group or community affair, questions of cost and gain can be completely overshadowed by cosmological meanings of corporate ritual symbolism.

Calculated economics do not account for the conventional symbols and the expressiveness of ritual sacrifice which are the primary concern of the papers in this volume. Sometimes the economic element falls away altogether when something valueless is offered: a wild cucumber by the Nuer, for example, or a wafer of bread and a cruet of wine in the mass. Religious ritual sacrifices do not necessarily incorporate a calculation of loss and gain.

Turning to the other side of the dichotomy, a calculated material sacrifice can take on religious characteristics. When a person gives up the economic rewards of a promising career for the benefit of his family or of a political cause, his vision of what makes life meaningful and worthwhile is dramatized and communicated. Such a sacrifice may be central to a person's beliefs and values, and it certainly expresses them. Although it does not necessarily involve the prescribed use of conventional symbols which comprise the ritual sacrifices discussed in this volume, a significant material sacrifice for a cause highlights a theme that ritual sacrifice can express, namely, the subordination of lesser goods to an overriding ideal.

The idea that sacrifice involves giving up some material good for the sake of an ideal has a parallel usage (possibly its origin) in Christian religious contexts, when voluntary ascetical practices (like giving up sweets for Lent) are referred to as sacrifices. The usage arises from an emphasis on the Gospel theme that the ultimate expression of Christ's acceptance of his divine Father's will was his voluntary acceptance of suffering and death. An emphasis on this theme has often resulted in a very negative understanding of sacrifice, seen as giving up something desirable, and therefore the antithesis of pleasure and joy. This does not reflect the observations of ethnographers. Although sacrifices can be performed with reluctance and sorrow, more usually religious sacrifices are occasions of celebration and joy. The costs, if considered at all, are met with willingness, even liberal pleasure.

Prestigious Killings

There are certain types of ritual killing which are sometimes called sacrifice, but with which we are not primarily concerned in these studies. One such type could be called 'prestigious sacrifice'. In the North American institution of potlatch, for example, Kwakiutl men used to vie for status by the amount of property consumed and destroyed at the feasts they gave; in the case of a very important man, animals and sometimes slaves were killed. Another example is the burial of important men among several West African peoples, in which survivors show their respect for, and display the importance of, the deceased by the number of animals and people (or heads) to be buried with him. Such institutions differ from the religious rites with which we are primarily concerned in that the former are concerned with status, a material benefit, rather than with cosmology and meaning for life: prestigious killings do not contain such themes as consecration, release of power, cleansing from evil, and others, which, as Beattie points out in his contribution to this volume, are so common in religious sacrifices.

Nevertheless, prestigious killings do dramatically express the relative values of the people performing them. They communicate the idea that, compared with the person being honoured, even human life is trivial. Such dramatic acknowledgment of the status of an honoured person is a theme which may be found among others in religious offerings to supernatural powers.

Execution of a Criminal

Another type of ritual killing which has characteristics in common with sacrifice is the execution of a criminal. Although in modern societies, execution is defended as a pragmatic way of coping with particularly serious cases of deviance rather than as a ritual expression of beliefs and values, some aspects of capital punishment can be associated with sacrifice. An execution is normally surrounded by ritual which prescribes procedures before death, the manner of the killing, necessary witnesses and functionaries, and so on. These rituals serve to safeguard the value normally given to human life by removing the execution as far as possible from the informal running of everyday activities. Capital punishment also dramatically expresses the horror felt by the community of the crime for which the convicted man has been condemned, and it reinforces the values which the crime has challenged. This is especially the case when executions are performed publicly. Capital punishment definitively removes from the community a person who is thought to be so depraved as to be capable of such an offence. These ideas have parallels in the themes of religious sacrifices which we shall be discussing.

A further link between capital punishment and sacrifice arises when the demand for capital punishment expresses a reaction to community fears, often the result of a state of general lawlessness. The extension of capital punishment in England in the eighteenth century was partly the result of an inability to cope with the incidence of crime; and in contemporary emerging countries, increasing crime often brings similar reactions. The result is that just when the general state of society suggests mitigated culpability on the part of individuals who commit crimes, the punishment is made more severe. Convicted criminals die on account of something much wider in society than their particular crimes.[9]

The execution of a criminal comes closest to religious sacrifice when the crime is believed to be an offence against a deity, and the community is prepared to give up one of its number (the guilty person) to appease the offended god. An example from the Shona people of Zimbabwe is the execution by burning of the man believed to have caused drought by seducing the virgin consecrated to a powerful rain god: the execution was carried out under the direction of religious and political authorities, in a grove sacred to the spirit, and it involved the co-operation of the important lineages of the chiefdom in their appropriate roles (Bourdillon 1979). This ritual act is not distinguishable from the apotropaic sacrifices mentioned in Beattie's contribution.

The idea that ritual can protect community values which are otherwise threatened is reflected in other religious sacrifices. It is significant that the Nuer, among some other pastoral peoples, may kill their cattle only in sacrifice and consider it very degrading to kill merely for meat except in time of severe famine: even then an invocation to the spirits precedes the killing (Evans-Pritchard 1956: 263—71). More generally, Beattie draws attention to the idea that sacrifice involves the destruction of right order in the death of a human being or a surrogate for one. Ritual has the effect of separating and isolating a series of actions from the ordinary processes of life. What is otherwise forbidden becomes legitimate in, and only in, the sacred ritual context.

Sorcerous Sacrifice

This is a third type of ritual killing which, though much closer to religious sacrifice than executions or prestigious killings, can be distinguished by its being private and exclusive, and devoid of all social and moral values. Sorcerous sacrifices are performed in secret, by an individual or clique, for their own private ends, without any consideration for the good of the community as a whole. Typically, such a sacrifice involves an offering to an amoral or immoral tutelary spirit in exchange for some favour which the spirit is supposed to confer. And typically, such sacrifices are offered by persons considered to be evil witches or sorcerers, which enables us conveniently to classify them as sorcerous sacrifices. The controlling influence of community values is irrelevant to such a transaction, and often something of value to the community, perhaps even human life, rather than to the individual performing the sacrifice, is offered.

The French anthropologists, Henri Hubert and Marcel Mauss, in 1899 considered it a defining characteristic of sacrifice that it concerns, directly or indirectly, the moral person (see 1964: 13). Whether they are performed to strengthen a relationship with supernatural powers, or whether they comprise an attempt to be rid of evil influence, religious sacrifices in some way express moral values. Even when a religious sacrifice is performed privately and for private ends, it reflects community values, including a common assessment of what can legitimately be given up for the end required. More commonly, however, sacrifices are public, and serve to strengthen social ties as well as the beliefs and values of the community.

This is not to assert that the boundary between religious and sorcerous sacrifices is always clear. Private interest, such as curing illness, is often prominent even in religious sacrifices, which are in accordance with communal moral values. There is no *a priori* way of deciding what constitutes a clique as opposed to a moral community: what appears to one group of people to be a defence of legitimate interests, may appear as evil witchcraft to others who are opposed to the first group. Besides, in many societies there are ambiguous persons, believed to have power for both good and evil, whose sacrifices to appease troubling spirits can have an equally ambiguous nature: these are illustrated by what Bishop Arinze (1970) calls 'joyless' sacrifices offered by the ambiguous Ibo diviners to evil spirits. Some of the symbols of sacrifice discussed by Beattie, especially the release of power through death, are relevant to sorcerous sacrifices. Nevertheless, the anti-social and immoral nature of, for example, ritual murders associated with the powers of witchcraft, make them significantly different from the religious sacrifices which are the primary interest of the authors of the essays presented in this volume.

As do executions, sorcerous sacrifices highlight the contrast between what is done in the ritual context, and communally accepted normal behaviour. In each case, the ritual context isolates the action from ordinary life and categorizes it as in some way extraordinary; but the results in the two cases are different. In the case of execution, society believes that its normal values are protected by ritually isolating an execution. The fact that the executioner may kill someone in controlled ritual circumstances does not free him to kill in any other circumstances. In the case of sorcerous sacrifice, it is believed that the sorcerer ritually protects himself from the normal consequences of his crime: through ritual, the habitually evil sorcerer frees himself from social restraints.[10]

Dramatic Threat

E. Westermarck (1908: 618—24) pointed out that sacrifices have often been performed to convey a threat or curse, and that such sacrifices are distinct from religious sacrifices. Evident examples were sacrifices performed to confirm a treaty or an oath in the ancient Middle East[11], which took the form of a dramatised conditional curse: 'if you break faith, may you suffer this' (cf. McCarthy 1963: 55). One ancient Assyrian treaty contains the following passage:

> Just as male and female kids . . . are slit open and their entrails roll down over their feet, so may the entrails of your sons and daughters roll down over your feet . . . Just as they burn an image of wax in the fire . . . just so may your figure burn in the fire . . . (cited in McCarthy 1963: 76—7).

This is powerful symbolic drama. It could be argued that such sacrifices are religious in that they confirm or impose obligations, possibly moral obligations; and very often deities are called upon to witness the action and implement the threat in the case of a breach of faith. Nevertheless, the symbolism that the Assyrian words convey is closer to that of the curses of sorcery (which, however, are not conditional) than to the worlds of meaning expressed in religious sacrifices.

Religious Sacrifice

In contrast to the various kinds of sacrifice we have been considering, religious ritual sacrifices are those which through dramatic symbolism express fundamental beliefs and values.

I have still not defined sacrifice. Beattie points to the difficulty of finding a suitable definition, and confines his comments to rituals which involve the immolation by death (at least symbolically) of a living being. Most of the essays presented in this volume presume that this is the principal denotation of 'sacrifice'. Since the way in which people understand their rites are as important as the actions they perform, we include under the category of sacrifice rituals in which immolation by death is symbolically represented: Campbell-Jones argues that the Mass as performed in the convents she studied is to be properly understood as sacrifice. (In the mainstream of Christian theology, however, this understanding is modified, a point that is discussed in the Postscript to the essays.) We also have an account of sacred offerings of food in an Indian community which contain a number of features in common with animal sacrifices: Hayley's study illustrates themes of gift offerings, of consecration, and of a sacred meal, themes which are central features in the study of sacrifice.

III. INTERPRETATIONS OF SACRIFICE

A number of interpretative theories of sacrifice have appeared in the literature. Although no overall theory of sacrifice has yet proved entirely satisfactory, some of the more significant theories have provided useful themes in the interpretation of sacrifices. I suggest that each theory brings out the prominent theme in a particular type of sacrifice,[12] and that the variety of theories presented in the literature derives from the variety of sacrifices performed in different cultures and in different situations.

A Gift of a Deity

Sir Edward Tylor (1871) proposed a theory that sacrifice evolved from the idea of giving a gift to a deity as if he were a man. Tylor argued that the most suitable way in which the object can be transmitted to a deity is by reducing it to the form of smoke, which is related to the primitive idea of the nature of spirits. Beattie comments on some of the limitations of a gift theory of sacrifice, and Tylor's evolutionary speculations of how various kinds of sacrifice derived from such a primitive form are without foundation. Nevertheless, the idea of offering a gift to a god is a central feature of many religious sacrifices. This is particularly evident in rituals which primarily involve the offering of a libation to spiritual powers, with the killing of an animal or fowl as an occasional extra (as is the case in many Shona rituals). In such sacrifices, the victim must be first consecrated, but there is little emphasis on killing the victim or shedding of blood. Food and drink may be redistributed to those present, following the manner in which an important person would redistribute gifts of food and drink with which he had been honoured. This kind of gift giving is well illustrated in Hayley's contribution on Indian rituals.

Notice that gifts connote for anthropologists an element of exchange; when people offer gifts, they normally expect at least an equivalent return in kind or in service or in status. The gift confirms a relationship with mutual obligations. Sacrifices conceived as gifts can involve open exchange, in which the deity is expected to confer general protection and favour; or the sacrificial gift may involve closed exchange, in which the gift is offered in order that the deity may confer a defined benefit, such as health or a safe journey or fulfilment of the nefarious designs of a sorcerer.

Beattie comments on the theme of a gift as part of oneself, a theme which can be applicable to sacrifice in varying degrees between two poles or types: a gift of oneself, and a gift at someone else's expense. Examples of the latter are many sorcerous sacrifices, in which the sorcerer attempts to gain supernatural power at the expense of others. North American sacrifices of enemy captives and a variety of royal sacrifices can also be considered sacrifices in which the beneficiary does not give of himself. A sacrificial offering of oneself in a literal sense is rare. A clear example (if it happened that way) is the case of Decius Mus of ancient Rome who is said to have rushed in ritual attire to be slaughtered among the enemy in an offering of himself to the gods, to gain victory for the city (Livy 10:28). Less explicit (but better authenticated) examples might be the death for his country of a Japanese suicide pilot, or the burial alive of a Dinka religious leader which I shall be discussing shortly.

A third type of gift is a token gift, in which the offering has no value except as an expression of intent and good faith. An example is a Nuer offering in sacrifice of a wild cucumber, which is called an ox, possibly with the intention of offering a real ox when the time is more auspicious (Evans-Pritchard 1956: 203).

In many sacrifices, however, the idea of a gift is of secondary importance, and in some it is totally absent. Even when the idea of gift offering is present, we should not too readily apply the model of gift-giving between people to offerings made to gods: Hayley warns us that a theistic interpretation of Hindu religion can distract from the concern with purity and religious power which is central to the food offerings she describes. A scapegoat, sacrificed to remove evil or impurity from a community, is in no sense a gift offering; neither are many sacrifices performed to release some kind of impersonal power. I suggest that sacrificial gifts be considered as a class of sacrifice. The class is not exclusive, for the theme can be found in conjunction with others; but sacrifices which can be interpreted primarily as gift offerings can be distinguished from other kinds of sacrifice in which other themes are emphasized.

Ritual Control of Death

Sir James Frazer (1890) produced a theory of sacrifice out of the ritual killing of a 'divine king.' He claimed that originally an unsuccessful priest-king was sacrificed when he was believed responsible, directly or indirectly, for some calamity such as drought or famine from other causes (1911: 344—67). This in Frazer's view was extended to the killing of an ailing king who was no longer able to represent the life of the people; and subsequently to many other types of sacrifice. Frazer admitted that the killing of a god is not common, but presumed that it had once been more widespread and since forgotten by many peoples (1913: 226—7).

Although such a presumption cannot now be taken seriously, Frazer's linking of sacrifice to his theory of 'divine kingship' is not without interest. We have already noticed that execution can in certain circumstances become a religious sacrifice. Here I wish to draw attention to cases in which an ailing 'divine king' is killed in order to prevent a natural and uncontrolled death. The best ethnographic account of such a ritual is R. G. Lienhardt's (1961: ch.8) discussion of the burial alive of a Dinka priest-chief. This was performed as an honour to an especially important leader, at his own request, in the belief that he was responsible for the life of the community and must not lose control of his own life in a natural death. Lienhardt shows how that ritual could in fact renew the militant self-awareness of the people.

As ritual can transform homicide into legitimate execution, here ritual transforms the death of an ailing leader into something auspicious, and under his control. The death is taken out of the context of everyday events, and placed instead in the sacred context. The Dinka chief is not to be mourned. He does not die like other men. He willingly brings an end to his life for the good of his people.

Frazer's suggestion that other sacrifices arose from attempts to find a substitute for the divine king—and subsequently, substitutes for the substitutes—can help us to interpret some scapegoat sacrifices and, for example, the human sacrifices to strengthen the monarchs of ancient central African kingdoms. Frazer's theory, however, can be applied only to a limited type of sacrifice.

Substitution

E. Westermarck (1906: 65—6; 1908: 604—26) suggested that the origin of sacrifice lay in attempts to find substitutes for persons whose lives were in danger, and E. O. James (1953) developed this theme in relation to a wide variety of sacrifices. It is certainly a strong implication in a wide range of sacrifices that life is destroyed in an offering to a god in order that others, or another, be restored. This is most evident when a sacrifice is offered to restore to health someone who is seriously ill, or to ward off some serious threat to the community. In these, as in sacrifices to remove defilement, Beattie points to the importance of the theme of substitution, which he links to an interpretation of gift-giving. We cannot, however, presume that when a life is offered to a deity it is thought of as a substitute for some other life: not all sacrifices show evidence of such an interpretation.[13]

Substitution is clearly an important symbol in the sacrifice of a scapegoat, in which evil is eliminated from a community, not by executing or exiling guilty persons, but by symbolically conferring guilt or pollution on to a sacrificial victim which is then killed or driven out of the community. Although this appears to be a very different kind of rite from the offering of a beast *to* a deity, it is still a religious sacrifice in the sense that a life is given up, and it does affect the moral state of the people for whom it is performed.

Ritual Meal

W. Robertson Smith (1899) was wrong in his theory that sacrifice evolved from a totemic meal. But it would also be wrong to ignore his observation that, in some rituals, the killing of an animal is incidental to providing a meal at which the participants are believed to communicate with a deity. An example is the ancient Jewish paschal meal which seems once to have been associated with the sacrifice of a lamb. A ritual meal forms a central part of many other sacrifices.

There are two significant aspects of a community meal performed in association with sacrifice. One is a sharing of food to symbolize and enhance the unity of the participants. This is an application of the widespread symbol by which social relationships are expressed and controlled in eating and drinking together. The other aspect of a sacrificial meal is communion with a deity. To eat food that has been consecrated and offered to a deity is frequently believed to bring the participant closer to the source of supernatural power. In some forms the deity is symbolically consumed in the sacrificial meal. Symbolic access to divine attributes in a ritual meal is illustrated in this volume by the Hindu rites described by Hayley, and both aspects occur in the different interpretations of the Eucharist discussed by Campbell-Jones.

Clearly the meal is not essential to sacrifice. Rogerson mentions ancient Hebrew sacrifices in which the offering was entirely burnt; in others the flesh of the victims was consumed only by priests. Commensality goes against the symbolic logic of many 'disjunctive' sacrifices, where the victim becomes the symbol of all that is undesirable.[14] Among other peoples, the flesh of victims is eaten outside the sacrificial rites (see, for example, Evans-Pritchard 1956: 274 on Nuer sacrifice). On the other hand, Hayley's essay shows how communion with the supernatural may be effected through a sacred meal without the ritual killing of an animal. It could therefore be argued that communion is a separate kind of ritual and should not be confused with sacrifice. Nevertheless, the ritual killing of a domestic animal, and in some cases of a human, is a particularly apt occasion for a sacred meal, which is a central feature of many sacrificial rites. The material presented by Hayley highlights a theme which cannot be divorced from a study of sacrifice.

Power

Beattie and Dieterlen indicate sufficiently the importance of some kind of power to be released or removed in sacrifice. Here I wish only to draw attention to the ability of sacrifice to express and confirm a particular type of power, namely political power. The power of a king over the lives of his subjects is dramatically expressed by human sacrifices performed in his honour. This is how Bradbury (1973: 75) interprets the frequent human sacrifices in the traditional kingdom of Benin. A similar, but less dramatic, theme can be discerned when the property of subjects is forcefully abducted for royal rituals, as when a black ox of a commoner was stolen and sacrificed in Swazi royal rituals (Kuper 1947: 199).

IV. NATURAL SYMBOLS IN SACRIFICE

Symbols, and the rituals which embody them, are manmade and conventional. A symbol can usually be interpreted only in and for the culture in which it occurs. There are, however, certain symbols which contain the same range of meanings among widely differing peoples, suggesting that in these cases there is a natural association between the symbols and their meanings. Thus V. W. Turner (1966: esp. 80—1) has pointed out widespread symbolic characteristics of three basic colours, white, red and black, which he suggests are related to important bodily products: white is the colour of semen and of mother's milk; red is the colour of blood—maternal blood, or blood shed in war or in hunting; black is the colour of faeces and of bodily dissolution (though I suggest that darkness is a more significant association for black). From these facts, natural symbolic meanings for the colours suggest themselves. The question arises over the degree to which sacrifice uses natural symbols rather than arbitrary cultural symbols.

Since sacrifice is so widely used as a central religious ritual, it would seem in this sense to be a natural symbol. On the other hand, since it contains so many different themes and different interpretations, any natural association between the act of ritual sacrifice and its meaning is not at all clear. In fact, there are a number of natural associations between different aspects of sacrifice and various meanings it can communicate. The following are some of the more important aspects of death and killing which have natural and frequent symbolic uses in sacrifice.

Death is Final and Irrevocable

This has relevance for sacrifices which solemnise a change of status or an action; also for the theme of a gift to a deity in which the offering must no longer be available for one's use.

Death Involves the Destruction of Vitality

This has possible interpretations in the release of power and the removal of power. In sacrifices where the victim is bled to death, vitality is readily associated with blood.

The end to Life is the end to the Conscious Self

This consideration makes life the most profound offering a person can make. Self-sacrifice is ultimately expressed in death, and dramatically expressed in the death of a symbolic substitute.

A corollary of the last point is that the destruction of human life is the destruction of the moral person. This is relevant to the sacrificial killing of a guilty person, and makes sacrifice a ready symbol in situations where people feel a need to remove something evil or defiling.

A second corollary is that to kill someone is the ultimate harm one can do him. A wish or threat of death can be dramatically expressed by killing a surrogate.

Death is a Precondition for a Carnivorous Meal

This fact links sacrifice to all the symbols of commensality.

Ultimate Political Power Includes Power to Kill

This is relevant to certain sacrifices in connection with royalty. It also helps to explain the widespread association between death and power, especially in sorcerous sacrifices.

Destruction of Property Expresses Relative Values

This happens in two possible ways. What is destroyed is considered of less value than a benefit expected, as in calculated, non-religious sacrifices; and a greater value is emphasized by belittling what is destroyed, as in prestigious killings. These factors make sacrifice a ready tool for expressing moral and religious values.

Domestic Animals often have some special association with People

This is a cultural, rather than a natural, phenomenon; but it is very widespread, and often there is a certain equivalence between domestic animals and people expressed in brideprice payments or in blood compensation. This also is relevant to the theme of substitution.

Any of these features, or any combination of them, may be significant in the interpretation of sacrifice in a particular context, besides a multitude of culturally specific symbolic themes. Any general theory of sacrifice is bound to fail. The wide distribution of the institution of sacrifice among peoples of the world is not due to some fundamental trait which fulfils a fundamental human need. Sacrifice is a flexible symbol which can convey a rich variety of possible meanings.

V. THE CONTRIBUTIONS

The essays in this volume do not claim to provide a general theory of sacrifice. Nor do they provide detailed descriptions of exotic destructive rites to titillate the curious. They offer ways of analysing and interpreting a highly adaptive religious symbol.

Beattie outlines ideas which are currently influential in anthropological thinking on sacrifice. He looks at the kinds of question an anthropologist is likely to ask in the study of any particular sacrifice, and he outlines the basic pattern which commonly occurs in sacrificial rites, together with some of the social functions sacrifice commonly effects. Beattie goes on to probe an area which is fundamental to religious ritual when he considers sacrifice in its relationship to the release of, and release from, different kinds of power. He shows how different conceptions of the power concerned, and different relationships to it, result in fundamentally different kinds of sacrifice.

The volume moves on to the Judaeo-Christian tradition with Rogerson's study of Old Testament sacrifice, which is largely cautionary in tone. There are many very different sacrifices recorded in the Old Testament. A certain unity achieved by later Christian allegorizing is largely illusory. Although anthropologists have given attention to the Old Testament, and although Old Testament scholars have readily turned to anthropological writings for help in interpreting their material, we do not in fact have the detailed social data concerning the peoples of the Old Testament that make possible the depth of analysis normally considered appropriate to social anthropology. This lack is not crucial to theologians, who, as Rogerson suggests, are more concerned with stories recited than with their social background.

Sykes takes us into the New Testament and the specifically Christian tradition. This involves moving one's attention away from specific rites, and turning it instead to a more general 'world of meaning'. He shows how a concept of sacrifice, which is derived from the Old Testament stories about particular sacrifices, is central to the way in which the New Testament writers understood the events recounted in the Gospels. The method of analysis differs from anthropological approaches due partly to the data available, and partly to the difference of aim between anthropology and theology. Detailed social background and context is not available for the New Testament documents; instead, the literary tradition allows an analysis of meaning in the context of thoughts of the individual writers, and of the corpus as a whole. The emphasis must accordingly move from the ritual experience of participants to the normative thinking of religious leaders.

Sykes goes on to argue that the sacrificial language of the New Testament writers attempts to express a fundamental paradox in human life, a paradox that is not specifically Christian. This feature of the paper goes beyond a descriptive analysis of the sacrificial language of the New Testament. In a typically theological manner, it attempts to show that the historical symbols maintain a wider interpretative usefulness.

One significant feature of New Testament interpretations of sacrifice is that they use Old Testament stories and symbols, but give them a new and adapted meaning appropriate to the Christian context. This has a parallel development in non-Christian Jewish writings which in various ways interpreted the Aqedah, the Old Testament story of the sacrifice of Isaac by his father, as a primal sacrifice from which others take their meanings. A brief survey of this tradition is presented in Hayward's appendix to Sykes's paper.

In contrast to Sykes's theological analysis, Campbell-Jones presents an anthropological study of Christian symbols in practice. She is not concerned with what a systematic theologian may present as a Christian world of meaning. In this study, we see how certain contemporary Christians variously interpret their ritual sacrifices. The essay adds a further dimension to the study of sacrifice by showing that different interpretations of sacrifice can be related to varying patterns of social life.

Hayley provides an example of an anthropologist at work in the analysis of ritual. A detailed knowledge both of the rituals and of the socio-cultural context in which they occur enables her to interpret for the modern western reader how the Assamese understand their rites. She warns against to ready an application of preconceived theory and preconceived concepts. The food offerings are not to be understood simply in terms of the social structure of the caste system (as some authors have tried to understand them); and western theistic ideas can be very misleading when applied to Hindu religious concepts.

Although the rites she describes do not include animal sacrifice, her analysis of how the Assamese become purified, and partake of the nature of the gods, through making a consecrated offering from which the devotees subsequently eat, illustrates a characteristic of most religious sacrifices. The analysis makes and illustrates the significant point that the experience of the rite is an end in itself. Through the performance of the food offerings and subsequent meal, people feel the effects of devotion, purity attained and spiritual power released.

In the Postscript, which is suggestive rather than conclusive, a view of Christian sacrifice in the contemporary world is presented. It suggests how contemporary Christians may still find a place for this symbol in interpretation and ritual. Sacrifice as a key symbol in the Christian world of meaning depends on the variety of possible interpretations which anthropologists point to, and which prevents any single anthropological theory from embracing the whole range of sacrifices that comes before them.

NOTES

1. Raymond Firth (1964: esp. 206—24; also 1961: 183—214) argues in favour of a 'value-free' discipline. The idea that anthropology challenges established morals is widespread, expounded, for example, moderately by Firth and less moderately by E. R. Leach (1968b). Berreman offers a good case for the more committed approach of the radicals, in which he comments, 'We believe that neutrality on human issues is simply not an option open to anthropologists.' (1969: 89.) For a discussion of the relationship between anthropology and ethics, see Edel and Edel 1968; also Ladd 1957. Cf. also Westermarck 1932.

2. Schleiermacher, the father of liberal protestant theology, was the earliest and most influential person to attempt to ground theology in human experience and to emphasize its role in the re-interpretation of traditional forms of expression. For a contemporary exponent of this kind of approach, see Wiles 1974. Pannenberg (1976) takes a less radical position, while still rejecting a 'metaphysical' approach to the subject.

3. An important exception is in the study of healing rituals, which anthropologists accept as being often efficacious. For a recent discussion on this topic, see Moerman 1979 and accompanying comments.

4. An example is provided by the group of South American 'liberation' theologians, the fruits of whose discussions were published in the series, *A Theology of Artisans of a New Humanity*. For them, the sacraments of the Catholic Church are about community relations, and their efficacy can be judged only in terms of these relationships (cf. Segundo 1974: ch. 3).

5. Cf. Segundo's (1974: 63) depiction of magic as 'a matter of looking for devine efficacy in certain procedures without any relations to historical efficacy. In the last analysis, magic is the absence of historical realism.'

6. Such ideas are put forward in various ways by, among others, C. Lévi-Strauss (1960: 53), M.-H. Piault (1975) and M. Bloch (1977—see my response in Bourdillon 1978).

7. There is no reason to believe that the Aztecs were more deprived of protein than their neighbours, and in any case descriptions of the rites suggest that the expense incurred in pampering the victim prior to sacrifice makes an economic explanation very dubious. See Sahlins' response (1978).

8. Robertson Smith (1927: 395) argues that the 'introduction of ideas of property into the relations between men and their gods seems to have been one of the most fatal aberrations in the development of ancient religion'. He was at least correct in his observation that economic considerations were not a central feature of most ancient sacrifices.

9. Radzinowicz (1948) gives an account of the use of capital punishment in eighteenth-century England. His descriptions of procedures of public executions, and of crowd reactions at them, suggest that more was involved than simply retribution for crime. Westermarck (1932: 189) argues that executions 'to avenge god's anger', a principle acted upon by Christian governments until quite modern times, amount to human sacrifices.

   One particular execution which is of particular interest to this collection is the execution of Jesus of Nazareth. Sykes in the present volume depicts this as a sacrifice from the point of view of his followers, but does not advert to the various sacrificial characteristics it may have had for the executioners. Apart from the general connection between execution and certain types of sacrifice, in this case there is evidence of trumped up charges. Frazer (1913: 412—23) speculates on the parallels between the gospel accounts of the mockery of Jesus and other accounts of the ritual killing of an effigy of Haman.

10. An interesting related theme is found in Euripides' play, *Iphigenia in Aulis*. The only person whose character appears unscathed is Iphigenia herself, and there is a link between Menelaus' willingness to sacrifice his daughter and his decision to lead the Greeks to war for the sake of a whore.

11. In the 'Taxonomy of Sacrifice' I presented to the conference, I referred to such sacrifices as examples of 'sacrifices of solemnization'. This was partly based on dubious ethnography (cf. Rogerson's 'additional note'). In fact, people use whatever is available from their store of communal ritual in order to give solemnity to an occasion: when sacrifice is a dominant ritual in a particular society, it is likely to be used. 'Solemnization', therefore, refers to a type of social situation, rather than to a type of interpretation of sacrifice.

12. The elucidation of prominent themes has some similarity to van Baaren's (1964) listing of root forms of sacrifice. He lists four such forms: gift offering; renunciation for the benefit of another; repetition of a primordial event; symbolic sanctification. The list is not exhaustive, and the last two forms are not peculiar to sacrifice.

13. Middleton (1960: 100), for example, claims that the idea of substitution is not to be found in most sacrifices of the Lugbara of Northern Uganda.

14. See Beattie on p. 38 ff. for an explanation of the term 'disjunctive'.

ON UNDERSTANDING SACRIFICE

J. H. M. Beattie

I

In what follows I try to set out what seem to me to be some of the more interesting problems to which the study of sacrifice has given rise in recent social anthropology. This will involve some reference to work in this field by contemporary—and some earlier—anthropologists. But what is intended is not an inventory of the various theories that have been put forward, but rather a sort of propaedeutic, an attempt to determine what questions may most usefully be asked, and what kind of answers may be looked for.

The first thing to do is to decide, approximately at least, what we are to mean by the term 'sacrifice'. To say that the word is an ambiguous one is an understatement. I am reminded of a celebrated discussion of 'totemism' by the American anthropologist Goldenweiser (1932), who showed, many years ago, that there is no single criterion by which the concept might be defined which is not lacking in what is taken to be 'totemism' *somewhere*. 'Sacrifice' is in much the same case. So I shall not attempt to define it precisely. It will be best to begin by setting out a rough approximation, and to move on from there.

In Latin, the word 'sacrifice' means, of course, 'to make holy or sacred'. Now what, to begin with, do we mean when we say that something is made holy or sacred? How can we change something into that condition? We would reply, I suppose, 'By consecrating it by some such rite as the laying on of hands, by dedicating the thing concerned to God or the gods, or by blessing it.' As Hubert and Mauss put it in their justly celebrated essay on sacrifice (a work to which I shall be referring again), 'In every sacrifice an object passes from the common into the religious domain; it is consecrated' (1964: 9). The reference here is to the distinction between the sacred and the profane—a presumed polarity to which much importance was attached by Durkheim and his followers, though it has since come in for some criticism.

My own view, and I think that of some others, is that if the distinction is somewhat reformulated, and taken to refer to aspects or even contexts of things, rather than to 'things' themselves, and if it is interpreted as distinguishing between the empirically-based, 'technical' aspects of experience on the one hand, and its symbolic, expressive aspects on the other (Durkheim at least hinted at this, though of course for him social values were what was symbolized by and expressed in religious ritual—see Lukes 1975: 242—3), then it is still valuable. What seems to happen—or at least one of the things that seems to happen—in, for example, the consecration of an animal for sacrifice is that the animal is made into a symbol. And we must remember that symbols are man-made; they are 'unnatural' rather than 'natural': they are not to be found lying around like pebbles on a beach. And whatever else a symbol is, it is essentially and by definition something that stands for, 'symbolizes', something else. (There is more to it than that, of course, but this will suffice in the present context.)

At once the question arises: what, then, in sacrifice does the thing sacrificed stand for or symbolize? And here the answer, one which is supported by much modern ethnography, seems to be that it stands for (probably among other things) the person or persons who are making the sacrifice or upon whose behalf the sacrifice is being made. As Marcel Mauss pointed out long ago, in giving a man gives, albeit in a metaphorical sense, part of himself, and in the ritual offering made in sacrifice to a god or spirit a man is likewise symbolically giving part of himself. And as Evans-Pritchard puts it in writing about the Nuer of the Southern Sudan, 'in sacrifice . . . some part of a man dies with the victim' (1956: 280).

But it is important, especially in the context of sacrifice, to remember that the sacrificer's gift of himself is not literal; it is the ox or sheep or chicken that is killed, not he. And, for the Nuer, it is the *life* that is forfeited and made over to God (to whom, they believe, it belongs anyway); the meat remains to be eaten by men. In sacrifice a man is saying that he wants something, and in order to obtain it he is making a vicarious sacrifice of himself. But it is *vicarious*; he is, it is fair to say, managing to have his cake and eat it too.

Our next question is, what is sacrificed? Usually, and ideally, another living creature, precisely because, being living itself, it most appropriately symbolizes the life that is being offered. The living creature that best represents the person or group of persons for whom the sacrifice is made is no doubt another human being, and human sacrifice, though never an everyday occurrence, is familiar to us from many ages and cultures. But most usually in blood sacrifice the life of an animal is offered, almost always that of a *domestic* animal, cow or ox, goat, sheep, chicken. Why is this? Because, it seems, domestic animals are identified with the home, and with the human group that lives there; with *man*, as against 'nature'. They can therefore most appropriately symbolize the humans on whose behalf the sacrifice is being made. But sometimes, since luckily human beings, and gods too, may be willing to compromise, a token offering may be made, for example a vegetable offering instead of an animal one. Thus if a Nuer does not happen to have an ox available he may sacrifice a species of cucumber instead. But he asks God to accept an ox, not a cucumber (Evans-Pritchard 1956: 280). It is not that he thinks that God is so stupid as not to know the difference; it is rather, I suspect, that he knows that what he is performing is a rite, a drama, and not a commercial transaction; his gift, that is to say, is symbolic, not 'real'. It is the thought, the intention, that counts, as we (and perhaps the Nuer also) might say.

In this essay, I follow Evans-Pritchard (1956: 197) in excluding from consideration in the context of sacrifice such practices (closely associated |though they are) as the pouring of libations, the offering of food and drink at shrines, and so on, also the dedication of living beasts to particular spirits. Like sacrifice, these are certainly types of symbolic gift-giving, made by men to spirits, and it may seem arbitrary to exclude them. But they do not include what for our purposes it is useful to regard as the central feature of sacrifice, the killing, immolation, of a living victim. For we shall see that this, or an act symbolizing it, is usually the central and most important element in the sacrificial ritual, and it is this aspect of it which has always seemed especially to call for explanation.

To whom, or to what, is sacrifice made? Sometimes, as among the Nuer (and the ancient Hebrews) to a High God, variously conceived. Sometimes, perhaps more usually, to lesser divinities and spirits believed to be able to affect man's condition. Very often, especially in Bantu Africa but of course elsewhere too, to the ghosts of the dead, either individually or collectively. But—and here again we see something of the complexity of the topic—sometimes the 'gift' aspect, the idea that the sacrifice is *to* somebody or something, is very much played down, or even disappears altogether. The sacrifice may be conceived as not really *to* anything, the emphasis being rather on getting rid of something; 'evil', 'sin', ritual pollution, or whatever. Here we encounter the familiar theme of the scapegoat, an idea which seems to play a part in most sacrifices. This is an important issue, and I return to it below.

It would be possible to consider here further such basic and preliminary questions, for example *when* do people sacrifice and *who* does the actual sacrificing? I pass over these questions now, not because they are unimportant, but because they are usually fairly easily answered from the ethnographies. Usually people sacrifice at times of personal or group crisis, or periodically, as advised by the diviners, for the general good. And the sacrificers may be priests, senior members of the family or lineage, the sufferer himself. These questions can only be answered, in particular cultures, by looking at the evidence.

These bare bones (so to speak) may give us at least a minimal, preliminary notion of what we are to be talking about. We know, to begin with, that we are concerned with a rite, not with a piece of empirically-grounded technology: I shall return to this point, which is an important one. We know that there has to be a victim, and that the idea of communication with a god or gods, or with other spirits, may be (though it need not be) involved. This communion may, or may not, involve the idea of commensality, a shared meal. We know, also, that sacrifice may be thought to involve a change in what Radcliffe-Brown called the ritual status of the participants; this may be conceived either as an access of spiritual power from outside, or as the removal of a dangerous power ('pollution') which is afflicting them. I shall return to this point also. This list is very far from exhausting the possible aspects of sacrifice. The notion is, as is already plain, an exceedingly complex one, and there is no way of knowing beforehand just what sacrificial ritual in a particular culture may involve. One has to look and see. And as always the important thing is to have some idea what to look for, what the possibilities are.

Before I try to set out these possibilities as systematically as I can, let me say a few words about the basic point that sacrifice is a *rite*. This means, as we have noted, that in sacrifice something is being *said*, as well as done. No more than any other ritual is it to be understood as nothing but a piece of mistaken technology, of pseudo-science, based on a false conception of the nature of things, as Frazer and his latter-day followers would have us believe. What seems to underlie the institution of sacrifice, in all its many forms (and I admit to some over simplification here), is a reference to a non-empirically grounded *power* or *powers*, whether this 'power' be thought of as a kind of individual, but non-human, 'personality' ('personalized', if the term may be permitted), or not. The idea of such powers is not based on any kind of experimental procedure; it is rather a dramatic, symbolic expression of man's awareness of his dependence on forces outside himself. And ritual, including sacrificial ritual, provides a means of influencing, or rather of hoping to influence, these forces. What underlies ritual is, I believe, the notion that the symbolic, dramatic expression of something may *work*. Causal efficacy is imputed—though not as a result of conscious decision-making—to the symbolic expression itself. One is reminded of the American anthropologist Robert Redfield's appealing definition of magic: 'magical rites are little pictures of what one wants' (1962: 436). An observation by the sociologist Peter Berger, writing about a survey carried out in Western Germany, is also relevant here. In his survey sample, he reports, '68% said they believed in God—but 86% admitted to praying' (1970: 40). An implication of this rather surprising finding would seem to be that the effectiveness of the act of praying does not entirely depend upon whether or not someone is listening; for at least a substantial number of West Germans it would appear that the rite of prayer is somehow thought to be effective in itself.

What I am suggesting is that sacrificial ritual, like other rites, is a form of art, a drama, which is believed by its performers (when they reflect on the matter) to work. And as, in a sense, a language—a way of saying something as well as of doing something—it requires its own specific kind of understanding.

II

Before going on to examine more closely what we may call the ideology of sacrifice, let us take a quick view of sacrifice from the point of view of what actually happens. We need not be deterred by the fact that 'what actually happens' is of course itself in part at least a mental construct—what we, or others, *think* happens. If we are to stop and examine the epistemological implications of all the categories we use, we shall end up like the centipede which began to worry about which foot went after which; in the end it was unable to walk at all. Certainly we cannot say much about what people do *unless* we take some account of their ideas, what they think about what they do. But let us for a moment look at sacrifice as performance, before turning to the cosmologies and classifications that may or may not be involved. It has been justly said by Edmund Leach, following Marett and others, that 'the rite is prior to the explanatory belief' (1968a: 524). In a general sense, most people act out their rituals first and philosophise about them afterwards.

Evans-Pritchard (1956: ch.8) distinguishes four main acts or stages in Nuer sacrifice, and although not all of them may occur even in the Nuer case, his account is one of the most detailed we have and it provides a useful starting-point. First, the animal to be sacrificed (for the Nuer, ideally an ox) is tethered to a peg and *presented* to God. Next comes *consecration*, discussed above; for the Nuer this involves the rubbing of ashes from the family byre on the animal's back—a rite which not only 'sacralizes' the animal, but also identifies man and ox in the sacrificial context. In a sense, Evans-Pritchard writes, 'what one sacrifices is always oneself'. Third comes *invocation*, in which the officiant addresses God or Spirit at greater or lesser length, explaining what the sacrifice is for, and filling in the background. And finally comes *immolation*, the slaughter of the victim. Among the Nuer this is done by spearing it in the side if it is an ox, by cutting its throat if it is a sheep or a goat.

Let us look a little more closely at the last two of these stages, invocation and immolation. For the Nuer, invocation includes prayer, but it also includes a good deal of declamatory speech-making about various aspects of the social situation which led to the sacrifice. As Evans-Pritchard (1956: 211) puts it, it is an assertion, a statement of what is desired, rather than a supplication. Of course prayer is widely associated with sacrifice, and ethnography provides numerous examples. A recent paper by Fortes (1975) offers several detailed samples of the prayers which accompany sacrifice among the Tallensi of Northern Ghana; the pattern is similar throughout much of Africa and elsewhere. I have already mentioned the expressive aspect of prayer; Fortes brings out well its cathartic quality. By a bringing into the open of the state of affairs, which probably involves someone's presumed but unacknowledged negligence or misdeed, the air is cleared; which amounts to a kind of public confession. The idea that somebody's fault, a sin committed and unatoned, lies behind the misfortune—such as an illness, which the sacrifice is intended to remedy—is of course a very widespread one.

The immolation of the victim is generally the climax of the rite. Here Hubert and Mauss (1964: 9) anticipate much later theory when they speak of the 'religious energy' released by the sacrifice. For what occurs in sacrifice is, in their words, 'a crime, a kind of sacrilege', that is, the destruction, the murder even, of a human being or a surrogate for one (p.39). And it is because of this very fact that a new and ambiguous force is believed to be released. Death is in some sense an anomaly, a disruption, a breach of right order. And as such it is or may be a source of power. One is reminded of those human sacrifices supposed to have been carried out in the interlacustrine kingdoms of East Africa (and of course elsewhere) 'to strengthen the king'. The death is conceived of as releasing a kind of power of which others may avail themselves. I shall return to this topic when I discuss the Dogon, below. Here I wish only to draw attention to the widespread belief that the anomalous, the destruction of right order, may itself be a source of danger, and so of power, at least for those qualified by birth or training to receive it. The African witch who strengthens his —or her—power by committing incest, the crime which above all others typifies the anomalous and the disorderly, is a case in point. Another is the institution of royal incest itself.

Commensality, or eating together, is very often the concluding phase of sacrificial ritual, though only very rarely, I think, in the sense of the participants 'sacramentally eating their god', as Robertson Smith, inspired by the recent discovery of totemism, argued in 1889. Among the Nuer, the shared meal after the sacrifice is a purely secular affair, not itself part of the ritual. But it is common in some societies, including many Bantu ones, for the ghosts or spirits to whom the sacrifice is offered, when they are 'possessing' their accredited mediums, to share a meal with the living. In Bunyoro, a former Bantu kingdom of Uganda, a person possessed by a ghost (probably that of a deceased relative) to which a goat has been sacrificed—that is to say, in Nyoro representations the ghost itself—may in the course of a shared meal be given small pellets of millet porridge to eat by the others present, and may itself feed others in the same manner (Beattie 1964: 140).

But it would be a mistake to think that a shared feast is a universal part of sacrificial ritual. As so often in anthropological matters, sometimes it is and sometimes not.

Before I turn to consider the more 'structural' features of sacrifice, I want to mention, very briefly, one or two of its 'functional' aspects. Though for some contemporary anthropologists 'functionalism' has become a pejorative term, in fact the institution of sacrifice, like other ritual institutions, does have consequences as well as meanings (if not the consequences usually ascribed to it by its performers). The investigation of these consequences is certainly neither banal nor illegitimate. Here I wish to make, very briefly, three connected points.

First, sacrifice, whatever its other consequences, provides a dramatic performance for its practitioners and witnesses: as such there is no doubt that it can be a worthwhile and rewarding experience in its own right. This has been noted by many observers. Evans-Pritchard, for example, remarks of Nuer sacrifice that the sacrificer 'is acting a part in a drama', and he writes that when looking at a Nuer sacrifice 'we seem indeed to be watching a play or to be listening to someone's account of what he had dreamt' (1956: 280, 322). I have myself made somewhat similar observations in regard to Nyoro spirit seances, in which prayer and offering of food and drink play an essential part.

But perhaps the dramatic aspect of sacrificial ritual is best brought out (at least in African ethnography) by Victor Turner. He develops the idea of a dramatic cycle, including blood sacrifice, in the context of his analysis of the culture of the Ndembu of Zambia. The process is cyclic because the end sought is a restoration of a disrupted *status quo*. What is aimed at is 're-achieved amity and co-operativeness, with the hope of restored health, prosperity and fertility'. The means to this end are the enactment, through ritual, of the 'whole process of crisis and redress', through 'the symbolization and mimesis of traditional causes of trouble and feelings associated with it'. And sacrifice constitutes what Turner calls the 'high spot' in the drama (1968: 276).

Second, from the functional point of view, and following on from Turner's point, the cathartic element in sacrifice needs to be mentioned (I have already touched upon it in the context of prayer). The dramatic expression and working out, through the ritual, of the participants' anxieties and sense of guilt may enable them to get things off their conscience, so to speak. This will become plainer when we turn, shortly, to the piacular, expiatory aspects of sacrifice. Sacrifice is often thought of as a way of eliminating evil. And to *feel* purged of malignant forces in oneself is, in some measure at least, to *be* purged of them.

Thirdly—and this point also follows on from the preceding one— sacrifice is a social event, and it has social consequences. As Hubert and Mauss put it, 'the act of abnegation implicit in every sacrifice, by recalling frequently to the consciousness of the individual the presence of collective forces, in fact sustains their ideal existence' (1964: 102). It is but a short step from this formulation to Durkheim's classic analysis of 'primitive' religion, according to which through religious ritual 'the group periodically renews the sentiment which it has of itself and of its unity' (1915: 375). This is the formula which Radcliffe-Brown (1922) applied, with little if any modification, in his analysis of the ritual institutions of the Andaman islanders.

III

Other functional interpretations of sacrificial ritual could be advanced, but I turn now to what is probably the most interesting problem of all: that of understanding sacrifice from the point of view of the part-cipants, as far as this is possible. What do *they* see as its purpose, and what are the categories, the ways of thinking about reality, which are implicit—sometimes indeed quite explicit—in *their* view of the matter? There is in fact bound to be some overlap between 'our' view and 'theirs' (whoever 'we' and 'they' may be), if only because of our common humanity—and blood sacrifice is no less a part of the religious tradition of the Christian West than it is, today, of that of a traditionally-minded Nuer. In this context, however, we must be particularly on our guard against uncritically reading our own ideas and categories into the probably very different ways of thought of unfamiliar cultures.

It is important, I think, in this connection, to stress that when we are looking at sacrifice from the sacrificer's point of view we are looking at a relationship between two entities one of which, at least from our point of view, is 'real' (i.e. living people), and the other of which (ancestral gods, ghosts and spirits, impersonal powers, etc.) is, most of us would say, 'imaginary', in the sense that it comprises symbolic constructs of the culture concerned. The French anthropologist J.-P. Colleyne makes the point clearly in discussing Hubert's and Mauss's work. They proceed, Colleyne writes, 'as if they themselves believed in the mental representations they study' (1976: 38). The point is valid; confusion may indeed result if the anthropologist unguardedly follows the people he studies in assuming—or seeming to assume—the real existence of the various non-human powers and forces involved in their cosmologies. Such an assumption may, for example, tend to preclude the asking of important but difficult questions about how far, and in what sense or senses, the people themselves 'believe' in the literal existence of the entities concerned. For there may be degrees, or levels, of 'belief'. Of course if we follow some contemporary relativists, who hold that truth is relative to cultural context (so that to impute falsehood to beliefs held in other cultures is to commit a category mistake—a very bad kind of mistake), then these problems cannot arise. But I think that they do arise and that they are of special interest. This is why it seems to me to be essential, whatever the epistemological difficulties involved, to distinguish 'what happens' from 'what people think happens'. For what people think happens, and the categories in which they think it, are central concerns of many modern social anthropologists.

Bearing in mind, then, these cautions and provisos, we turn now to the problem of understanding sacrifice from this point of view.

So regarded, it is, I think, correct to say that almost always sacrifice is seen as being, mostly, about *power*, or *powers*. Power is, of course, a central theme in much traditional African thought. In 1945 Father Tempels claimed that the Bantu concept of personality (he was generalizing from the Baluba of present-day Zaire, among whom he worked as a missionary) involves the notion that 'force is the nature of being, force is being, being is force' (1959: 35). Tempels may have a little overformalised Luba philosophy, but in essence he is right. Power, force, energy, however we name it, is a concept of central importance in all human cultures, not just in Bantu ones, though it may be, and is, differently represented. So we need not be surprised that this is what sacrifice is thought to be chiefly about.

Now, let me make two distinctions. First, the power or powers with which sacrifice is concerned can be considered as being of two kinds. On the one hand, there is the power manifested in more or less personalized spiritual beings, ranging from a High God (often remote and otiose), through ancestral and other ghosts, to a variety of lesser spirits and powers. On the other hand, power may be conceived as a kind of impersonal, diffused quality or force, inhering in certain things and conditions; like almost all power this can be thought of as either dangerous or beneficent, or both. *Mana*, and the whole range of pollution concepts, fall into this second category. Of course there may be difficult borderline cases, and both of these kinds of expression of power may, and very likely will, occur in any given sacrificial complex. But as each may involve very different ideas about what the sacrifice is to achieve, it is essential to distinguish them. This is the first of our two distinctions.

Now for the second. As well as distinguishing between two kinds, or expressions, of power, we must distinguish between two kinds of attitudes towards, or intentions regarding, these powers. First, the object of the sacrifice may be to acquire closer contact with, or more of, the power concerned. Whether it be conceived as individualized or diffuse, in this context it is thought of as beneficial. Or, secondly, the intention may be apotropous or (in Evans-Pritchard's term) apotropaic (1956: 275), aiming at the turning away of, or separation from, the spirit or power in question. This distinction corresponds (approximately) to that made by Hubert and Mauss (1964: ch.2) between rites of sacralization—involving the *entry* into the person sacrificed for of the special sacred power or quality involved—and rites of desacralization, involving the *exit* from the person sacrificed for of the 'sacred' quality or potency concerned. It will be simpler, I think, to follow Luc de Heusch in designating this distinction by the words 'conjunctive' and 'disjunctive', terms which are, as he says, both more general and less ambiguous (in de Heusch (ed.) 1976: 39).

These two distinctions, between 'power' conceived either as individualized and personalized or as diffuse and impersonal, and between attitudes to it in sacrifice as either conjunctive or disjunctive, provide us with a fourfold classification of types or aspects of sacrifice, as defined by the conceptions and intentions of the participants. These are:

1) Sacrifice to obtain or maintain closer contact with God or with other individual spirits.

2) Sacrifice to achieve some degree of separation from such spirits.

3) Sacrifice to acquire for the sacrificer (or for the person sacrificed for) an increase, or input, of non-personalized 'power'.

4) Sacrifice to achieve separation from, or the removal of, such diffuse force or power.

These four categories, though distinct, are not necessarily mutually exclusive: elements of any or all of them may appear in the same complex sacrificial situation. But they do conveniently accommodate four of the main types or aspects of sacrifice with which we are familiar from the literature. Let us consider each of these separately (and briefly).

Into the first category fall all those sacrifices which involve the idea of communion, or commensality, the sustained relationships often implied by spirit mediumship, and so on. The idea of god-eating, thus making the god or spirit part of oneself, the theophagy central to the Christian Mass, fits in here. So does Robertson Smith's theory of sacrifice, already referred to, according to which the god and his worshippers partake of a sacred feast in which they eat the totemic clan ancestor, that is, their God himself. This theory—for which, as Evans-Pritchard pointed out, there is not a shred of evidence—was partly taken over by Freud, in his myth of the rebellious sons who killed and ate their tyrannical father. Whatever the psychological significances of such myths, there is no need to take account of them here.

But ethnography provides plenty of examples of such 'conjunctive' sacrifices. According to Fortes (1959: 30), writing about the Tallensi, the ancestor cult, which entails sacrifice, ' is the transposition to the religious plane of the relationships of parents and children', and it would seem fair to assume that in such relationships conjunctive elements far exceed disjunctive ones. This is plain, also, from the texts of some of the Tallensi prayers already alluded to. Comparable observations might be made in regard to some—not all—relations with the spirit world in Bunyoro. In particular, a sort of tutelary spirit called the *Mucwezi w'eka*, not in fact an ancestor spirit, is conceived as a kind of protective agent, charged with the well-being of the household (*eka*). The Cwezi are the spirits of a pantheon of ancient hero-gods, the objects of Bunyoro's traditional mediumship cult. Sacrifices may be made periodically to such spirits, which are said to 'purify the household, to protect it, and to bring it blessing' (Beattie 1969: 161). In these instances the emphasis is evidently on close and sustained contact, rather than on separation. A similar relationship of closeness and dependence on the spirit world, and especially on the ancestors, is widespread throughout Bantu Africa—and of course elsewhere. An elderly Sotho bishop in a

Zionist-type church in Sowetu, South Africa, is reported to have said:
'Although we are Christian we cannot drop our old fathers. We cannot
do it' (West 1975: 200).

It should, however, be stressed that relations with the spirit world
tend to be ambivalent, which is perhaps what we should expect. Conjunctive and disjunctive elements may occur in the same situation. But
of course this does not mean that it is not necessary to distinguish them.

The importance of spirit mediumship in this connection is that if
possession by a spirit is *sought*, the aim is necessarily conjunctive and not
disjunctive. Spirit is conceived as entering, even if only temporarily,
into the closest possible association with its host medium. Mary
Douglas interestingly contrasts the Nilotic Dinka and Nuer in this
respect. She writes that 'for the Western Dinka, the state of trance is . . .
a central cult, the source of blessing and strength. For Nuer, trance is
dangerous', and she goes on to relate this difference to other contrasting qualities of the two cultures (1970: 86—98). Communion,
symbolic gift-giving and commensality, and, often, spirit mediumship
are, then, characteristic elements in sacrificial ritual in this first of the
four categories which I have distinguished.

Turning now to the second category, where what is sought seems to
be disjunction rather than conjunction with the spirit world, the Nuer
again offer a ready example. For them, according to Evans-Pritchard,
the ghosts of the dead are relatively unimportant. Though he does
speak of 'dutiful sons' as honouring their fathers' memory by sacrifice
(1956: 161), he elsewhere expresses doubt as to whether sacrifice is ever
made to ghosts 'by themselves'; if they are referred to at all they
usually take second place in the invocations to God (1956: 201). In any
case, the Nuer attitude to the spirits of the dead is apotropaic: 'they ask
the dead to turn away from the living' rather than seeking closer union
with them. The apotropaic element also appears in sacrifice among the
Mandari (another people of the Southern Sudan). Jean Buxton reports
that in a sacrifice for a sick child the invocation addressed to the Spirit
of the Above and the ancestors included the words: 'We have cut a
goat for the ancestors and have dedicated a sheep and a lamb for the
Above; you must come out and leave us in peace and return to the
place of evil [i.e. westwards], and not bother us any more' (1973: 171).
The Bantu Nyakyusa's attitude towards the ghosts and the spirit world
is similar. The aim of Nyakyusa ritual, Monica Wilson writes, 'is not
that union with god constantly sought in Christian ritual, but a separation from both the shades and the heroes; for close association with the
pagan gods spells madness and death, not fullness of life' (1957: 204).

In the third and fourth of our categories the concern is not with gods, ghosts or spirits, a sort of quasi-persons, but with non-personalized ritual or spiritual power. First, let us look at the case where what is sought by the sacrificer is an increase or an input of such power. Here the most illuminating, indeed what must be the classic, instance of such a conception of the intention and effects of blood sacrifice is to be found in the work of what I may call the French school of Africanist anthropologists. Their founder was, I suppose, the late Marcel Griaule, and his researches, together with those of his colleagues and successors, among the celebrated Dogon of Mali, are rightly famous. I cannot do justice here to this work, which still continues, but a few quotations will, I think, sufficiently make my point.

It was Marcel Griaule who first introduced to us the Dogon notion of *nyama*, which he described as 'an impersonal, unconscious power (*énergie*), distributed in all animals, plants, supernatural beings and natural objects' (1976: 51). It is this power that is released in sacrifice, at the very moment of the death of the sacrificed animal. So, according to Griaule, sacrifice is a way, almost a 'technique' (and he uses this very word) for making use of a force, *nyama*, which is already in existence. As Luc de Heusch points out, contrasting the Dogon in this respect with the Nuer, 'the Dogon interpret the dangerous condition in which someone who has breached a prohibition finds himself as a *loss* of spiritual substance', and he goes on to quote Madame Dieterlen, also a pioneer in this field, as having shown that 'the effusion of sacrificial blood and the release of vital force that accompanies it have as the participants see it precisely the function of making good this loss' (1976: 13, 16). In Mme Dieterlen's own words (or rather in my translation of them) 'one of the functions of sacrifice [I here add the words 'as seen by the participants'] is that the current [*courant*] established by the effluxion of the victim's blood, and the release of *nyama* which accompanies it, can alleviate the lack which the person sacrified for is suffering from, and so help him to make good the loss of substance which he has undergone (1976: 45).

So for the Dogon, it seems, sacrifice does not really create anything; it is a way, almost a technique, for making use of a power or force which is already in existence. When thus released, *nyama* becomes a power for good. As is usual with the Dogon, the matter becomes more complex and subtle the further one goes into it; underlying all Dogon sacrifice, it seems, in a kind of inversion of the Christian story, is the idea of the immolation of the creator God, Nommo, himself. Through a mythical cycle of cosmic events, fully described in the ethnography, disorder is somehow converted into order. These are fascinating themes, but for my present purpose it is sufficient to report that for the Dogon (as no doubt for others) the diffuse, impersonal power called *nyama* is, in at least some of its aspects, beneficial to man. The bad ritual condition which the sacrifice is to remedy is due not to the presence of something, but to the lack of it. And this lack can (it is believed) be remedied by blood sacrifice. The Dogon attitude to sacrifice, and to the power which it is believed to release, is thus explicitly conjunctive.

Moving on, then, to our fourth category, perhaps more widespread in human cultures, in Africa and elsewhere, is the opposite notion to the Dogon's, the idea that a bad ritual state is due to the *presence*, not the absence, of an impersonal, potentially dangerous power. So the object of sacrifice is not to acquire more of this power, or closer contact with it, but to get rid of it. Under this aspect of sacrifice fall many of its most familiar features. Most important among these is its piacular intention, including the notions of expiation and atonement. The aim is, through sacrifice, to get rid of an evil power, presence or quality within oneself. This power has been differently conceived in different cultures, but in one form or another the idea of it seems almost universal. Pollution, sin, guilt, impurity, evil, even 'violence', are a few of the words which, in different contexts, have been used to translate it. Sometimes a vernacular term has been adopted because no word in Western languages seems to translate the concept exactly; the famous Polynesian *mana* is an example. A comparable idea is represented by the Bantu Nyoro by the word *mahano*, a mysterious, sometimes dangerous, force or power in certain, generally anomalous, things and conditions (Beattie 1960).

What is common to all of these terms is that they refer to something vaguely conceived as flowing or diffused, usually contagious, having a special potency, predominantly dangerous and potentially destructive. Its dangerous, inimical aspect may be situational; a power which is dangerous for ordinary men may be safely encountered by those qualified, either by birth or by expertise, to deal with it. And it may, in some of its meanings, be thought of as being brought about through someone's fault or sin, characteristically (but by no means only) by the crime of incest. Hence the link with the concept of guilt and so with the need for expiation and propitiation, and indeed with the very notion of 'punishment' itself.

But however it be conceived, it is usually (though not invariably—consider the fate of Oedipus) believed that the fatal, or potentially fatal, contagion *can* be got rid of, if the appropriate ritual is performed. And one such ritual is sacrifice. We saw that for the Nuer, the rite of sacrifice may involve the transfer of the evil in a man's heart into a sacrificial animal, through the rite of rubbing ashes on its back. To quote Evans-Pritchard again: 'Nuer say that what they are doing is to place all the evil in their hearts on to the back of the beast and that it then flows into the earth with the water or the blood' (1956: 280). The creature sacrificed is thus a substitute—a surrogate victim. As we noted earlier, it represents, stands for, the sacrificer, or the person sacrificed for, who is identified with it by the consecrating laying on of hands. So the evil is taken away from men, and disposed of by the death (or, what comes to the same thing, the banishment) of the surrogate victim. Evans-Pritchard concludes that this is the central theme of Nuer sacrifice. 'If we have to sum up the meaning of Nuer sacrifice in a single word or idea, I would say that it is a substitution, *vita pro vita* . . . Substitution is . . . the central meaning of the rites' (1956: 281—2). As we noted earlier, what one sacrifices is always, in a sense, oneself. (I need hardly add that Evans-Pritchard is not saying that we can, or should, sum up the meaning of Nuer sacrifice 'in a single word or idea'. Nobody has brought out more clearly than he has the numerous and complex ideas involved. In fact he lists fourteen of them: communion, gift, apotropaic rite, bargain, exchange, ransom, elimination, expulsion, purification, expiation, propitiation, substitution, abnegation, homage. And there are many more!)

Much could be (and has been) said about the expiatory, purificatory, piacular aspects of sacrifice; they link up, of course, with the familiar 'scapegoat' theme, mentioned above, in which the evil in men's hearts is transferred to a beast—or a man—which, if it is not killed, is driven away into the wilderness to die. Either way the principle is the same.[1] There are links here, also, with the witchcraft ordeals of some parts of central Africa (and of course nearer home), in which the evil of the community is conveniently located in convicted witches, whose elimination from that community purifies and purges it, at least for a time, of the evil powers which have been afflicting it. It may be suggested, too—in fact it has been suggested—that the continued support in some quarters of the ritual of capital punishment may be due to its affording, for some, a similar vicarious purification of the community.

Such conjectures are, however, outside my present brief. Let me conclude with a brief summing up.

IV

I began by considering how anthropologists have generally found it most useful to use the term 'sacrifice', and I followed some modern scholars in stressing its symbolic, expressive aspects. Then, with some reference to ethnography, I discussed what, in different cultures, actually happens in sacrifice; what people do. I looked briefly at what appear to be some of its social consequences or 'functions', whether the participants are aware of these or not. Next I considered some of the meanings, as these are stressed in different cultures, which sacrifice may have for the people who practise it. I suggested that these meanings and intentions could perhaps usefully be represented in terms of a fourfold classification. This was based on two considerations; first, whether spiritual power or powers were conceived in the form of distinct and individual gods and spirits, or rather as an impersonal and diffused force; and second, whether men's attitude towards them in sacrifice was conjunctive (aiming at closer contact) or disjunctive (aiming at separation). And I stressed throughout that although these and other aspects of sacrifice could usefully be distinguished for purposes of analysis, it would be a mistake to regard them as necessarily mutually excluding one another in the context of the sacrificial institutions of a given culture.

NOTE

1. For a recent and stimulating treatment of this theme, see Girard 1977. And see review by Beattie in *Royal Anthropological Institute News* **29**, December 1978.

SACRIFICE IN THE OLD TESTAMENT: PROBLEMS OF METHOD AND APPROACH

J. W. Rogerson

The aim of this paper is to acquaint social anthropologists with the most important of the traditions concerning sacrifice in the Old Testament, and to indicate the major problems of interpreting these traditions within the discipline of Old Testament study. By 'sacrifice' is meant those religious ceremonies in which an animal or bird victim was killed. Such ceremonies did not, of course, exhaust what may loosely be called 'sacrifice' in the Old Testament, but such a restriction of the subject will be appropriate to the discussion to which this paper is a contribution. In Old Testament Hebrew there is no one word which corresponds exactly to the English term 'sacrifice'. Perhaps the nearest general term is *Korbān*, but this can include offerings of gold and silver, as well as animal sacrificial offerings. A variety of terms is used in fact in Old Testament Hebrew, and they are traditionally translated as 'burnt offering', 'peace offering', 'sin offering', 'guilt offering', 'thank offering' and so on.

Four major difficulties face the Old Testament scholar who seeks to interpret the material dealing with sacrifice. First, although most of this material probably reached its present form round about 500 B.C., there lies behind the final form a history of oral and literary transmission going back over five hundred years or more. We are thus not dealing with a straight-forward block of synchronic material. As will be shown later, there are some internal inconsistencies within the traditions, and there is evidence from the historical books of the Old Testament that the burnt offering was a much more prominent sacrifice in the period 1,000—600 B.C. than the Old Testament regulations about sacrifice would suggest. A structural anthropologist might argue that this historical dimension, of which the Old Testament specialist is so aware, is irrelevant, and that inconsistencies are all excellent grist to the structuralist mill. For good or ill, such a suggestion will evoke little sympathy among Old Testament scholars.

The second major difficulty of approach is a comparative cultural one. It has long been accepted that ancient Israel's sacrificial practices had something in common with sacrifice as practised among her neighbours, and that they were even in some respects derived from them (cf. Dussaud 1921). Granted this, is sufficient known about sacrifice both in ancient Israel and in the ancient Near East to enable valid comparisons, and conclusions based upon the comparisons, to be made?[1] Functionalist social anthropology might well regard such an exercise as irrelevant, preferring to concentrate on the one system under investigation, but Old Testament scholars would see value in such comparisons. For example, in a classic treatment of the subject, the Israeli scholar Y. Kaufmann (1963: 560—74) contrasted pagan rituals of the ancient world with those of the Old Testament. In pagan rituals for healing, there was the idea that some sort of evil force needed to be expelled if health was to be restored. In the Old Testament, no such idea was to be found. Healing came from God, and offerings made after healing were in thankfulness and obedience to God.

However, Kaufmann's argument leads to the third problem, that of popular versus official religion. It is evident from the prophetic and historical books of the Old Testament that throughout the history of ancient Israel, many people followed false gods, and sacrificed to them. To what extent then do we have, in the Old Testament, material about sacrifice that a field-working anthropologist would have observed, and to what extent do we have the idealised system of later official orthodoxy? Finally, if, as is most probable, Old Testament sacrifices were accompanied by liturgies or invocations, either we do not have them in the Old Testament, or else they are there (perhaps in the Psalms) but we cannot recognise them as such for certain. In other words, one of the major ingredients of sacrifice as outlined in Beattie's paper is lacking in the case of the Old Testament.[2]

These problems have been mentioned in order to show that for Old Testament study at any rate the interpretation of sacrifice is not something derived simply from a knowledge of the content of the Old Testament. Ancient Israel existed in a particular cultural and historical milieu, and Old Testament literature both spans a thousand years and yet leaves much unsaid. These facts must be borne in mind as I now turn to give a brief outline of what the Old Testament actually contains on the subject of sacrifice. The first main block of material is Exod. 25—31 and 35—39. Most of this contains detailed instructions about the design and furnishings of the tabernacle and its courtyard, including the ark of the covenant. It also specifies the clothing of the priests, and gives details for the consecration of priests (Exod. 29:1—37) and the dedication of the tabernacle and its sacred objects. A daily burnt offering of two lambs, together with flour mingled with oil plus a libation of wine, is also commanded (Exod. 29:39—42).

The next main block is Leviticus 1—9, 12—17, 23. Chs1—3 deal generally with burnt offerings, cereal offerings and peace offerings; chs4—5 deal with sin offerings and 6:1—7:10 with guilt (or compensation) offerings. Chs8—9 describe the consecration of Aaron and his sons to the priesthood, while ch.12 describes the purification sacrifice for a woman after childbirth. The diagnosis of 'leprosy'[3] and a 'leprous' garment is explained in ch.13, to be followed in ch.14 by the sacrifices which rehabilitate a 'leper', as well as a 'leprous' house. Ch.15 deals with sacrifice for a person who has become unclean through a bodily discharge, for example, a menstruating woman. Then follows a famous passage (ch.16) dealing with the Day of Atonement. Ch.23 specifies sacrifices that are to be offered at the feast of unleavened bread, the 'waving of the sheaf', the feast of weeks, the (autumn) new year festival and the feast of Tabernacles.

In the book of Numbers, ch.6 specifies the sacrifices for a man who takes the vow of a Nazirite, ch.7 records the anointing and consecration of the tabernacle and its appurtenances by Moses after which a representative of each tribe offered in turn: a bull, a ram and a male lamb for a burnt offering; a male goat for a sin offering; and for peace offerings two oxen, five rams, five male goats and five male lambs. In ch.8 the Levites are consecrated, while ch.15 repeats general regulations about burnt offerings, peace offerings and sin offerings, adding to what is stated in Lev. 1—3, offerings to fulfil a vow, or freewill offerings. The ritual of the red heifer is described in ch.19. This whole burning of the heifer provided ashes which, mixed with living water (i.e. from a spring or river), were used in the ritual of cleansing any person who had had contact with a dead body or object associated with a dead body. In Numb. 28—9 we meet the fullest details about daily and festival offerings contained in the Old Testament, some of which appear to contradict the regulations in Lev. 23. For example, Lev. 23:18—19 prescribed for the feast of weeks seven lambs, *one* bull and *two* rams for a burnt offering, one male goat for a sin offering and two male lambs for peace offerings, while Numb. 28:27—30 prescribed seven lambs, *two* bulls and *one* ram for a burnt offering, and one male goat for a sin offering. Traditional Jewish interpretation of these passages denies the contradiction by saying that the texts refer to two different sacrifices (See Rosenbaum and Silberman 1944: Leviticus, 106a—106b).

The book of Deuteronomy is less concerned with the 'how' of sacrifice than with the 'where'. It constantly reiterates that sacrifice may be offered only 'in the place which God will choose' (cf. 12:5) and only in ch.21 does Deuteronomy give any detailed ritual, covering the case where an unsolved murder is expiated by the elders of the city nearest to where the victim's body was found. In Deut. 16:1—8, regulations about Passover are found which differ in important details from the regulations in Exod. 12:1—20. In the latter passage, the lamb is to be killed in such a way that its blood can be sprinkled on the lintel and door posts of the door of the house where the Passover will be eaten (Exod. 12:7, 22); and the flesh of the lamb is to be roasted. In Deut. 16:1—8, the lamb is to be killed and eaten at a central sanctuary ('at the place which the LORD thy God shall choose to cause his name to dwell in'——Deut. 16:6—7). There is no reference to sprinkling the blood on the lintel and door posts, and the flesh of the victim is to be boiled, not roasted. Such, indeed, are the differences between the two accounts that Jewish interpretation distinguished between the 'Passover of Egypt' and the 'Passover of the generations', regarding Exod. 12:1—20 as mainly concerned with what happened at the first Passover in Egypt, and Deut. 16:1—8 (together with some elements of Exod. 1—20) as dealing with subsequent observance of the Passover in the settled conditions of the land of Israel.

A further block of material dealing with sacrifice is found in Ezekiel 45—6, and can be dated to the period of the exile (587—540) when the Temple in Jerusalem was in ruins. It was a vision of a restored Temple, and deals with regular daily, weekly, monthly and festival offerings. Again, there are differences between this material and what is found at Numb. 28—9. For example, the daily offering of two lambs, one in the morning and one in the evening, specified by Numb. 28:3—8 becomes merely one lamb each morning in Ezekiel's vision of the restored Temple in Ezek. 46:13—15.

In addition to all this specifically cultic material, there are references to sacrifices throughout the 'historical' books of the Old Testament, the whole burnt offering being the sacrifice most commonly mentioned, and then in connection with momentous events. For example, burnt offerings were made by Noah after the flood (Gen. 8:5), by the men of Beth Shemesh using the oxen that brought back the art of the covenant from its Philistine 'captivity' (1 Sam. 6:14—15), by Samuel in the war against the Philistines (1 Sam. 7:9—10), by David when the plague upon Israel ceased (2 Sam. 24:22) by Elijah in his encounter with the prophets of Baal on Mount Carmel (1 Ki. 18:38), and by a non-Israelite, Mesha King of Moab, who offered his son so as to avert certain defeat at the hands of Israel, Judah and Edom (2 Ki. 3:27). Family festival sacrifices are mentioned in connection with David's family

(1 Sam. 20:29) and Elkanah's family (1 Sam. 1:4—5).

I make no apology for giving such a long outline of this material; it is necessary to know the area that is covered, so as to be wary of supposing that any one simple view of the meaning of Sacrifice can cover all these instances. Also, I must emphasise that my survey is not exhaustive, and has necessarily said nothing about the difference of ritual as between sin offerings for the priest or the congregation and sin offerings for a ruler and for an ordinary Israelite, one difference being that the priest's sin offering was burned outside the camp whereas the layman's sin offering was consumed by the priests in the holy place.

SIN OFFERINGS

	(Leviticus 4: 1—21) Priest, or the whole congregation	*(Leviticus 4: 22—6* *6: 24—30)* [Hebrew: 6: 17—23] Ruler	*(Leviticus 4: 27—35* *6: 24—30)* [Hebrew: 6: 17—23] Common person
Animal:	bullock	male goat	female goat or female lamb
Blood:	sprinkled 7 times before the veil of the sanctuary, and put upon the horns of the inner altar	put on horns of outer altar	put on horns of outer altar
Fat parts:	burnt upon the outer altar	burnt upon outer altar	burnt upon outer altar
Remainder:	burnt outside the camp	consumed by priest	consumed by priest

Of course, the earliest interpreters of these traditions, Christian as well as Jewish, faced fewer problems of interpretation than we do. They had the advantage of believing that the legislation had been disclosed by God on one occasion, and that there had been no historical development. Their main tasks was thus to explain and reconcile the various discrepancies between different accounts of the same festival. For example, Deut. 16:7 which orders the boiling of the Passover lamb was reconciled with the regulation in Exod. 12:7 that it should be roasted by the argument that 'boil' in Deut. 16 was the *general* term for cooking, which *included* roasting (Rosenbaum and Silberman 1944: Exodus, 54). Other ambiguities, and the discussions to which they led, have recently been highlighted by the publication at the end of 1977 of the Temple Scroll from Qumran. An interesting example concerns the Day of Atonement (Yadin 1977: 106—7).

At Numb. 29:7—11 the animals to be offered on the Day of Atonement include 'one male goat for a sin offering, beside the sin offering of atonement'. Lev. 16:5 says that Aaron is to take on this day two male goats for a sin offering. Putting together Numb. 29:11 and Lev. 16:5, the question arose as to whether there were to be three goats offered or two; whether the 'one male goat for a sin offering' of Numb. 29:11 was additional to or included in the two male goats of Lev. 16:5. Whereas Rabbinic opinion inclined to the view that there were to be two goats, the Qumran sectaries held that there were to be three. Whatever may have been the theory of the efficacy of sacrifice held among the Jews, it was enough that God had commanded the sacrifices, and that Israel should obey the commands. The discussion about the number of goats for the Day of Atonement, by the way, suggests that by the beginning of the Christian era the interpretation had become a matter of the interpretation of *texts* rather than interpretation of actual living rituals, since the Qumran community excluded itself from the Temple and its practices on the grounds of their profanity.

Christian interpretation of Old Testament sacrifice was necessarily allegorical from an early period. On the one hand, the sacrifice of Christ had summed up and rendered unnecessary all the sacrifices of the Old Testament; on the other hand, the details of all sacrifices, for example, those to mark the rehabilitation of the 'leper', could be interpreted in terms of the Incarnation and Passion.

The complicated procedure for this rehabilitation can be summarised as follows from Lev. 14.

1) The priest goes outside the camp to the 'leper'. He takes two live clean birds; cedar wood, scarlet and hyssop (probably so that the hyssop can be tied into a bundle and attached to the wood). One bird is killed over a vessel containing living water (the blood is then caught and mingled with the water), and the living bird and the 'bundle' are dipped into the blood and water. The 'leper' is sprinkled seven times and the living bird is released.

2) The 'leper' washes his clothes, shaves off his hair, washes his body and enters the camp. However, he remains outside his tent for seven days.

3) On the seventh day, he shaves off his hair, washes his clothes and bathes his body.

4) Final rehabilitation is effected on the eight day by anointing with blood from a guilt offering, and anointing with oil. In addition to the guilt offering, there are a sin offering and a burnt offering. Three animals (two he-lambs and one ewe-lamb) are

involved; but the ritual allows for a poor person, one he-lamb and two turtledoves or two young pigeons.

In early Christian interpretation of the ritual, the cedarwood points to the cross; the bird that is to die to the crucified humanity of Jesus; and the bird that is to go free to his divinity.[4] Even the 'leprous house' can be given a meaning within this scheme—for the house becomes the Christian faith, and the 'leprosy' in it is false doctrine.[5] Reformation interpretation of sacrifice, while being less allegorical and more concerned to describe the rituals themselves, nonetheless regarded Old Testament sacrifice as a synchronic scheme looking forward to the sacrifice of Christ.[6] It was not until the nineteenth century that the rise of source- and literary criticism became concerned with the history of Old Testament sacrifice, and, immediately, a totally different evaluation of the rituals emerged.

In his great classic *Prolegomena zur Geschichte Israels* of 1878, J. Wellhausen presented the following reconstruction of the history of Old Testament sacrifice backed by powerful arguments (1878: 53—79). The statements in passages such as Exodus 25—31 that Moses had instituted the sacrificial cult in obedience to the commandments of God on Mount Sinai were contradicted by passages such as Exod. 17:15, where Moses builds an altar *before* he reaches Mount Sinai. Moreover, the frequent prophetic denunciations of the sacrificial cult are unthinkable if this cult was widely believed at the time of the prophets to have been instituted by God on Mount Sinai. Ezekiel's *divergences* from the rituals prescribed in passages such as Num. 28—9 can only mean that Numb. 28—9 is *later* than Ezekiel, it being unthinkable that Ezekiel would propose a restored Temple following rituals *different* from what had obtained previously. The conclusion was that in the earlier period of Old Testament history (up to the seventh century), sacrifices had been spontaneous offerings, taking mainly the form of a sacrifice in which the worshippers shared the flesh of the victim in a communal meal. The seventh century saw a shift towards greater cultic regulation, culminating in the centralisation of worship by Josiah in 621. After the exile, and the rebuilding of the Second Temple between 539 and 516, this earlier spontaneity was replaced by regulations and commandments. Free-will offerings were not forbidden, but loyalty to God had now to be expressed by fulfilling the prescribed offerings. Sacrifice was no longer a family or clan matter centred around the fellowship meal; it was a national matter performed at the sanctuary. The daily sacrifices offered in the Temple, formerly financed by the king, were now financed by the whole people. There was now a concentration upon ritual defilement, and upon its expiation by the sin and guilt offerings. 'In the early period' wrote Wellhausen, 'the cult is like a green tree which grows up from the ground as it wishes and is able. Later, it is a tree correctly cut, always shaped with the help of compass and square' (1878:79—translation my own).

An important implication of this view of the history of Old Testament sacrifice was that the sacrificial cult of the Second Temple *did not represent the heart* of the religion of the Old Testament. The sympathies of Wellhausen and generations of (mostly Protestant) scholars who followed him were with the prophets who taught ethical monotheism, demanded social justice and denigrated the sacrificial cult. Passages such as Ps.51:16—17:

> For thou hast no delight in sacrifice;
> were I to give a burnt offering, thou wouldest not be pleased.
> The sacrifice acceptable to God is a broken spirit;
> a broken and contrite heart, O God, thou wilt not despise.

were held to represent the heart of the matter, while verses 18—19 of Ps.51

> Do good to Zion in thy good pleasure;
> rebuild the walls of Jerusalem,
> then wilt thou delight in right sacrifices,
> in burnt offerings and whole burnt offerings;
> then bulls will be offered on thy altar.

represented a late addition to the Psalm from quite a different standpoint.

To attempt here any discussion of Wellhausen's position, or of the question of 'spiritualisation'—that is, the problem whether Old Testament religion in some of its circles sought to substitute for sacrifices of animals purely *spiritual* offerings of contrition, prayer and thanksgiving—is quite impossible given the vastness and complexity of these issues.[7] It suffices to say that at this point our lack of knowledge of liturgies to accompany the Old Testament rituals is crucial. One recalls that in Evans-Pritchard's account of Nuer sacrifice, he describes how the sacrificers walk up and down before the victim, addressing the deity with lengthy invocations (1956: 209). If we could be *sure* that a Psalm such as 51 was a liturgy accompanying the bringing of a sin or guilt offering to the Temple, this would have important consequences for the history of Old Testament sacrifices and it interpretation. Critiques of sacrifice in the Psalms and prophets would be seen to be complementary to the rituals, and not in opposition to them.

It is now time to turn away from this general discussion of Old

Testament sacrifice, and to ask if we can discover what meaning or function the sacrifices had. In considering this, it is necessary to remember that in the sphere of wrong-doing, Old Testament sacrifices dealt not with deliberate offences, but with inadvertent ones. 'If any one sins unwittingly in any of the things which the LORD has commanded not to be done and does any of them . . .' says Lev. 4:2; and the passage then describes the various sin offerings to be brought, depending on the status of the offender. Some deliberate actions, especially deceit involving the property of others, were atoned by means of sacrifice; but this was only after the theft or whatever had been *fully restored* plus a fifth of its value. For actions such as murder or blasphemy, the penalty was death, and no sacrifice could avail (Exod. 21:12—17). In the famous story of David and Bath Sheba, David repented and Nathan the prophet declared that God had 'put away' (Heb. *he 'ebir*) his sin. Nevertheless, David was punished by the death of the child he had fathered, and by the tragic events of his subsequent reign (2 Sam. 11—12:25). If we wish to understand the scope of Old Testament sacrifice, it is probably best to operate with the distinction clean/unclean. If a person became unclean, he had to offer the appropriate sacrifice. He or she could become unclean in many ways: by menstruating or giving birth to a child, by contracting 'leprosy', by contact with a dead body, by unwitting transgression of a divine commandment, by deliberate deceit regarding the property of another. The distinction clean/unclean thus cut across the boundary that *we* would make between so-called ritual and so-called moral offences. (Clearly, the sacrifices that I am now discussing do not include free-will or vow offerings, or the daily sacrifices of the Temple).

Granted the need to remove uncleanness, how did the Old Testament sacrifices do this? Did the offerer transfer his uncleanness to the animal victim when he laid his hand on its head (Lev. 4:4)? Was it the sprinkling of the blood seven times before God in front of the veil of the sanctuary (Lev. 4:6) or the application of the blood to the horns of the altar (Lev. 4:7) that was efficacious? A good case can be made on the basis of Lev. 17:11 for the view that it was the application of blood to the altar that was effective:

> For the life of the flesh is in the blood:
> and I have given it to you upon the altar
> to make atonement for your souls: for it is the
> blood that maketh atonement by reason of the life.

Was the priest a 'sin-eater' on the occasions when he ate the flesh of the sin-offering? (Lev. 6:26, see Snaith 1967: 46). Do the bird that is let free in the cleansing of the 'leper' (Lev. 14:7), and the scapegoat that is led into the wilderness (Lev. 16:21—2), symbolise and effect the removal of uncleanness? All these suggestions have been prompted by the Old Testament material itself. An interesting suggestion based upon the distinction between the altars used in the various ceremonies has been made by J. Milgrom (1976: 237—8), with some support from early Jewish sources. He suggests that the effect of wrong-doing was to defile the Temple. If an ordinary Israelite were culpable, the cleansing was done by applying blood to the outer altar, the altar of burnt offering that stood in the Temple court. If a priest were culpable, the inner altar, the altar of incense in the tent of meeting was cleansed with blood, and in the case of the Day of Atonement on which the whole people was atoned for, it was in the Holy of Holies that the blood was sprinkled; in other words, the more important the offender, the closer to the heart of the sanctuary the cleansing.

Old Testament scholars have not failed to turn to social anthropologists for help in interpreting Old Testament sacrifice. The gift theory, to be found in the writings of Spencer and Tylor, was much used in G. B. Gray's posthumous classic *Sacrifice in the Old Testament* in the face of Robertson Smith's brilliantly attempted demonstration that fundamental to ancient sacrifice was not a gift to the deity, but communion with the deity through the communal meal.[8] In recent years, some social anthropologists, notably E. R. Leach (1976) and Mary Douglas (1966; 1975), have studied aspects of Old Testament ritual and sacrifice. As is to be expected, their approach differs from that of Old Testament specialists in being slanted towards an observer/structuralist interpretation rather than being participant/psychological.

In Leach's chapter 'The logic of sacrifice' from his *Culture and Communication*, two models are used to interpret *aspects* of Old Testament sacrifice. First, there is a model of significant space, in which This World, the Other World and a zone in which they overlap are realised in the various areas of the Temple/desert sanctuary. The Holy of Holies belongs entirely to the Other World, the Courtyard which admitted laymen belongs to This World, and between the 'lay' courtyard and the Holy of Holies is the over-lapping zone—the area containing the altars of incense and burnt offering. The second model is a 'rite of passage' model, in which the initiate or whatever is first ritually separated from society into a condition in which he/she exists outside of society for a short period of social timelessness, after which he/she is restored to society in the new role.

Leach makes effective use of these two models, even if as an Old Testament specialist I cannot accept some of his detailed points of interpretation.[9] First, his description of the consecration of Aaron and his sons in Lev. 8 fits well into the 'rite of passage' model. The ceremony is performed by Moses, who is assumed to have attained sufficient access to God already to be able to institute the priesthood. Aaron and his sons are 'separated' from the rest of the people by various rites including the putting of blood on their right ear, right thumb and right big toe. There then follows a period of seven days during which time Aaron and his sons are not to leave the door of the tent of meeting; this is their period of social timelessness. On the eighth day, their restoration to society in their new role as priests takes place with further offerings, the ceremony receiving the seal of divine approval when fire comes 'from before the LORD' upon the altar of burnt offering (Lev. 9:24).

Although he does not mention Lev. 14, Leach's 'rite of passage' model also works well for the rehabilitation of the 'leper', as was seen independently of Leach in an article by Douglas Davies (1977). In this case the 'leper' starts from being outside of society, and initial rites bring him to a period of social timelessness lasting seven days at the entrance to his tent. On the eighth day, he is restored to full membership of society, and, interestingly, the ritual at this stage includes as with the dedication of the priests, the putting of blood (and in this case oil) on the right ear, right thumb and right big toe (Lev. 14:14—18).

Both Leach and Davies discuss the ritual of the Day of Atonement (Lev. 16). Leach sees the ritual as a reversal of the process of anointing Aaron and his sons to be priests. Just as Aaron and his sons are separated from the secular that they might finish up ministering at the heart of the holy, so the 'scapegoat' starts in the sanctuary, and is separated so as to finish up outside the camp bearing the iniquities of the congregation.

Leach's explanation of the Day of Atonement in terms of the 'rite of passage' model is unconvincing because the ritual says nothing about the period of social timelessness elsewhere essential to this model, and it is not clear to me who or what is supposed to be changing its status. Leach seems to me to exaggerate in describing the scapegoat sequence as the 'exact converse of the Aaron sequence'. Douglas Davies's interpretation depends not on a 'rite of passage' model, but on the idea of different areas of holiness, beginning with the Holy of Holies, passing through the camp (the area of ordered social relationships) to 'outside the camp' (the place of disorder). The scapegoat, on this view, passes progressively from the sphere of the divine to the area outside of ordered relationships, symbolically bearing the iniquities of the society from its midst.

Studies such as the ones that I have been mentioning shed light on aspects of Old Testament sacrifice, and I have no doubt that it will not be long before we see Old Testament scholars employing similar approaches. By paying careful attention to the Israelite classification of the natural world, we shall get a better idea of how reality was structured for ancient Israelites into the holy, the ordered secular, and the disordered, and we shall be able to see how the sacrifices expressed and reinforced this system.[10]

Yet, having said this, let me emphasise that this does not mean that I regard the Old Testament material about sacrifices as in any way similar to 'a modern anthropological monograph', to quote E. R. Leach. The Old Testament material is *not* like the synchronic data observed and noted down by a field-worker. It has a history of many hundreds of years behind it, and comes from different strands of tradition. In order to emphasise further the point that we are not dealing simply with the interpretation of a synchronic system of rituals. I propose to conclude by mentioning a sacrifice (if it is a sacrifice) that is crucial to both the Old Testament and to Christianity: the Passover.

Modern critical scholarship is almost unanimous in its opinion that whatever the origin of the passover ritual (the killing of the lamb and sprinkling of the blood on the door posts), this ritual came to be linked with the narration of God's saving events at the Exodus from Egypt *after* this narration had assumed some sort of stable form in Israelite tradition (de Vaux 1964: ch.1). Many scholars argue that the ritual was originally an annual semi-nomadic rite, practised when the herdsmen moved from winter to spring pasturage. After the permanent settlement of these 'semi-nomads' in Canaan, the ritual was 'historicised' by association with the Exodus narrative. My own preference is for the theory of J. B. Segal, according to which the Passover ritual derives from a new year ceremony that would have been observed by the Israelites who were in Egypt (Rogerson 1978: 38—9). But whatever view one prefers, there is overwhelming agreement that the ritual is a sort of interpretation of the *story* of the Exodus deliverance, and that the recounting of the story was as important as the performance of the ritual. Indeed, the biblical material shows every sign of having been shaped by dramatic recitation: the plagues narrative builds up to a magnificent climax, and the narrative contains hints of rubrics in passages such as:

> And when your children say to you 'what do you
> mean by this service?' you shall say,
> 'It is the sacrifice of the LORD's passover,
> for he passed over the houses of the people

of Israel in Egypt, when he slew the Egyptians
but spared our houses'.
(Exod. 12:26)

By the time of the Inter-testamental Period, there had developed the
main parts of the passover Haggadah, the *recital* of the Exodus deliverance at a family meal. Significantly, after the exile, and possibly
earlier, the central feature of the ritual, the blood sprinkling, had been
modified in that the lamb was killed in the Temple, and its blood was
not applied to the door post and lintel of the house, but passed to the
priest nearest to the altar, and there disposed of (Mishnah Pesachim
5:5—6, in Danby 1933: 142). The lamb's only function was now to be
eaten at the communal meal. In the first century A.D., Rabban
Gamaliel taught that:

> whosoever has not said (the verses concerning)
> these three things at Passover has not fulfilled
> his obligation. And these are they: Passover,
> unleavened bread, and bitter herbs.
> (Mishah *Pesachim* 10:5, in Danby 1933: 150).

His words are often taken to refer to the obligation stated in Exod.
12:25—7 to explain to one's son the meaning of the service (Albeck
1954: 178). But D. Goldschmidt (1960: 50), in his introduction to the
passover Haggadah, argues that Rabban Gamaliel was alluding to the
celebration of the Passover in connection with belief in Jesus the
Messiah. If Goldschmidt is right, it is interesting that the Old Testament tradition as taken on into first century Judaism should see the
important difference between the two faiths primarily in terms of what
was *said*: whether the old saving acts at the time of the Exodus were
remembered, or whether the recitation centred around the story of
the passion of Jesus.

If the difference between Judaism and Christianity regarding the
Passover was focussed in the *story* which accompanied the ritual, this is
also a reminder that, ultimately, all sacrifices in the Old Testament
depend for their context upon the story of God's deliverance of his
people from Egypt at the Exodus. Whatever the origins of sacrifice in
ancient Israel, whatever their development in the course of Israel's
history, whatever light can be thrown upon them by anthropology and
comparative studies—and all these matters are legitimate subjects for
scholarly research—when the Old Testament is taken as a whole,
the context for understanding the sacrifices is the occasion when God
set out the law that his people should obey in response to their delivery

from Egypt. This highlights a fundamental difference between what a synchronic interpretation of Old Testament sacrifice might indicate to a theologian as opposed to an anthropologist. The anthropologist would presumably concentrate upon the structure and function of the sacrifices: insofar as he looks at the story it is only to elucidate a coherent system of symbols. The theologian would concentrate upon sacrifice as seen in terms of the story, and the insight into eternal reality which that story might contain.

NOTES

1. For a general discussion of the main problems involved in comparing Old Testament Religion with that of Israel's neighbours see most recently Saggs 1978.
2. In the discussion that followed this paper, Professor Fortes drew attention to Solomon's prayer at the dedication of the Temple (1 Kings 8:12—53). Whether or not this passage contains words actually uttered by Solomon on that great occasion, the passage is concerned entirely with the Temple as the earthly focus of the transcendent deity, and gives no clue about the meaning of the sacrifices that were offered in it. The most clearly identifiable 'liturgy' accompanying an offering is in Deut. 26:5—10, where the bringing of first fruits is linked with the story of God's redemption of Israel from Egypt, and the settlement in the promised land. See further, the conclusion of this paper.
3. 'Leprosy' is given throughout with inverted commas in order to indicate that the Hebrew word has a wider range of meanings than the English (see Driver 1963).
4. See the patristic evidence assembled by Cornelius à Lapide (1523: 717): 'Lepra est peccatum: haec expiator Primo, per lignam cedrinum, quod est fortissimum et imputribile, id est per crucem Christi, quae omnia vicet et superavit: Secundo, per coccinum, id est per sanguinem passionis Christi: Tertio, per hyssopum qua boni odoris est, id est per gratiam Spiritus Sancti, quae cooperatrix est emundationis nostrae: Quarto, per passerem vivum, id est per divinitatem Christi: Quinto, per passerem morientum, id est per humanitatem Christi immolata, huius enim morte vivificatur peccator: Sexto, per aquas vivas baptismi.'
5. 'Tropologice, lepra domus est corruptio fidei, vel morum in aliquia congretatione' (Cornelius à Lapide 1523: 721).
6. See, for example, Calvin on the purification of the 'leper' (1853: 19—28).
7. For a recent treatment of the subject see de Vaux 1964, Rendtorff 1967. On 'Spiritualisation', see Hermisson 1965.
8. Gray 1925. W. Robertson Smith in his *Lectures on the Religion of the Semites*, was, in fact, trying to uphold the view of the history of Old Testament sacrifice proposed by Wellhausen. See my article on *The Religion of the Semites* in the *Expository Times* vol. 90 (1978-79) pp. 228—33.

9. An unfortunate consequence of Leach's use of the Authorized Version of the Bible is that he thinks that Lev. 2 deals with 'meat offerings'—'a share of meat from a household meal is mixed with ritual oil and flour and frankincense, and handed to the priest' (Leach 1976: 88). 'Meat' in Lev. 2 is in fact an obsolete use of the word, and the offering has nothing to do with 'meat' in the modern sense. See Snaith, 1967: 46; Blunt n.d.: 130.

10. See the conclusion to Rogerson 1977. The warning note sounded by R. Bulmer (1973: 192) should also be noted: 'I am impressed by Dr Douglas's general theory of pollution, that this is associated with things that are out of place in terms of the order which a society seeks to impose upon itself and on the universe it occupies. But the trouble is that things can be out of place in so many different ways, in terms of so many different, even if linked, dimensions. The first problem, operationally, seems to me to be to ensure that the ethnographic record is comprehensively enough recorded and presented.' There can be little doubt that for the Old Testament, the ethnographic record is incomplete.

ADDITIONAL NOTE

At the conference, Michael Bourdillon provided a helpful 'Taxonomy of Sacrifice' (now incorporated in his Introduction to the present volume), which specifies 'the covenant sacrifices of the ancient Semitic peoples' in which the blood of a sacrificial victim was sprinkled on both parties to the covenant. In discussion, the question of Exod. 24:5—8 was raised, in which at the reading of the Book of the Covenant by Moses, blood was sprinkled upon the altar and upon the people. This passage, together with Deut. 27:7 has been interpreted as a covenant sacrifice, with the altar representing God as the other party to the covenant (see McCarthy 1972: 30, and the literature there given). Without entering into a very complex question, I must indicate my support for the view presented by E. W. Nicholson 1973: 72—4, in which it is argued that Exod. 24:5—8 is a rite of purification or consecration of the people, and that the applying of blood to the altar is the normal way of disposing of the remainder of the blood. As Nicholson says, 'it would appear that the only reason for believing that the altar in Exodus 24:6 represents God, is precisely the prior belief that the rite being performed was a rite of covenant ratification. Without such a presupposition there are no grounds for understanding the significance of the sprinkling of blood on the altar in such a manner.' (p.73). There were, of course, many ways in which covenants could be ratified in the ancient world, including ancient Israel, as is shown by McCarthy's examples on pp.41ff.

SACRIFICE IN THE NEW TESTAMENT AND CHRISTIAN THEOLOGY

S. W. Sykes

I

A sacrifice comes to notice as a specific act or a series of specific acts in a religious world of meaning. Because, however, religious worlds of meaning are plural and diverse, sacrifices are plural and diverse. The acts which are spoken of as sacrifices have sufficient in common with each other, or resemble each other sufficiently, to make it intelligible why they are spoken of as sacrifices; but there is no one thing which they all have in common, nor are all the resemblances and similarities of one type or degree. One may see why certain specific acts or series of occurrences are spoken of as sacrifices, but one will have the gravest difficulty in defining them. This familiar Wittgensteinian preface to the study of a complex topic uneasily unified under a general term is intended to undermine a long history of general theories about the nature of sacrifice; and in so doing it undermines also one type of religious apologetic, which identifies the *essence* of sacrifice and then interprets the preferred example as the complete expression of that essence.[1]

When faced with the extraordinary variety and complexity of what the modern social anthropologist has to reveal about the sacrificial rituals of different human societies, the first thing a Christian theologian must learn is to resist the temptation to try to create a basic structure to which they all conform. If social anthropologists themselves offer general interpretations, that is another matter. In this case there may well be a legitimate sphere for comment and appraisal; but apart from such critical activity, the Christian's interest in, and readiness to interpret, the sacrificial rituals of the religions of man has to be limited by certain important considerations. For example, contrary to some religious apologetic of the past it appears that sacrifice is *not* a universal religious phenomenon.[2] The Christian is not, therefore, in a position to say that the sacrifice of Christ (or the eucharistic sacrifice) expresses and fulfils the universally felt need of man to offer sacrifice to his gods.

Moreover, when he attends to the sheer variety of the rituals and their meanings the Christian non-participant must simple accept the ascesis of minute attention to the particular, regarding such attention not as a mere prolegomenon to grand theorising, but part of the homage of respect due to *persons*. The Christian interest, in short, is (or ought to be) less in the modern Western intellectual theories of sacrifice, than in the persons who sacrifice and their worlds of meaning; and the fruit of such attentions appears less in the approval of an intellectual élite, than in the assistance given to those who, in obedience to the command to preach the gospel to every creature, labour to establish a system of genuine communication between man and man.

These introductory considerations raise the question with some urgency. What sort of degree of commitment to sacrifice does the Christian have? The death of Christ itself was a judicial execution, not a ritual in the usual anthropological sense. On the other hand, the Eucharist is a ritual, which, with the dissent of Protestants, Christians generally refer to as a sacrifice, but with reference to the slaying of Christ.[3] The social anthropologist, not surprisingly, wants to know how the Christian uses the terminology of sacrifice. Is he saying that Christ's death is a real sacrifice (despite appearances), bringing all sacrifice to an end? Or are there continuous sacrifices being offered in the Eucharist? Or is the language of sacrifice merely used as a simile, to the effect that Christ's death (and the Eucharist) is *like*, but is not in reality, a sacrifice, so that all enquiries about the nature of sacrifice are, from the Christian point of view, of little significance?

The position which I propose to advance in this paper is that in the Christian world of meaning, sacrificial language is used realistically. The tradition is quite definite on this question. Thus St Thomas argues concerning the way in which the benefits of Christ's death were produced; 'It is clear that Christ's passion was a true sacrifice' (*Summa Theologiae* 3a, 48, 3). Calvin, likewise, distinguishing the sacrifice of Christ from sacrifices of thanksgiving consisting in the veneration and worship of God, and also from the Old Testament sacrifices of expiation and propitiation, affirms: 'They [*viz*, the sacrificial victims offered under the law] prefigured a true sacrifice such as was finally accomplished in reality by Christ alone; and by him alone, because no other could have done it' (*Institutes 4*, 18, 13). Although these two arguments are importantly different in character, and lead to two different types of theological apologetic, they agree in the essential point in question, namely that in Christian discourse Christ's death is spoken of a sacrifice realistically, and not as a simile.

Thus despite the fact that the public event of the slaying of Christ has the form of a judicial execution following a trial, its content is, at least as far as the central tradition of Christian thought is concerned, a sacrifice. It should be added that it is not *only* a sacrifice; as the language of the New Testament which we are to examine makes entirely plain, other terminology is also used. In fact, the Greek words for offering and sacrifice with reference to the death of Christ are neither prominent nor frequent in the New Testament, apart from their incidence in the letter to the Hebrews. The plurality of terms referring to the death of Jesus should not, however, be construed on the basis of a simple model of 'fact plus interpretation' (public death 'seen as' a sacrifice, a ransom, a judgement etc.); just as in the case of the sacrificial rites of other religions it is misleading to structure the sacrificial acts as 'slaughter of a domestic animal plus theoretical interpretation', as though the whole context of what occurs is not conditioned by the total meaning of each act in its occurrence. So, too, fidelity to Christian world of meaning requires that the events leading to, and surrounding, the death of Christ are laden with meanings, expressed in the intentions of the principal participants, not excluding those who thought they were disposing of a minor criminal.

A final introductory word must be said on the concept of metaphor. There exist what one must certainly identify as metaphorical uses of the term sacrifice.[4] To say that a man sacrificed his children to his career is not to make an observation belonging to a religious world of meaning. This remark is clearly metaphorical in the sense that the meaning of the concept of sacrifice is transferred from the religious sphere to that of family life, in such a way as to bring out the dimension of cost and suffering in the series of actions involved. It would be much *less* clear, however, if it were said the other way about; that a man sacrificed his career for his children.[5] Here, it might be said, because of the ethical dimension of voluntary self-sacrifice what takes place has a serious claim to be regarded as more than a sacrifice in a metaphorical sense. It might be felt that one who regularly put his children's basic interests before his own material advancement, whether as a religious act of self-abnegation or out of a sense of duty, has as much right to be regarded as offering a true sacrifice, as Agamemnon offering Iphigeneia. The issue is, what is the religious world of meaning in the context of which particular acts *are* sacrifices? The identification of a metaphorical use of the concept is logically dependent on the determination of the boundaries of religious worlds of meaning in which sacrifices appear as specific and significant acts.

The importance of this last observation will appear in the course of the essay. For here it will be argued that what is taking place in the

New Testament writings is the creation of a new religious world of meaning. In this context, which embraces new features, as well, of course, as transformations of old features, some uses of the concept of sacrifice appear to bear a 'metaphorical' meaning—that is, they seem to be best understood as a meaning-modification of an original subject (the death of Christ). But in reality, at least so far as the tradition is concerned, they are the foundations of a new world of meaning whose claim, as a whole, is to provide insight into reality.

II

There are three aspects of the way in which the sacrifice of Christ is understood in all the strands of the New Testament; these are (i) the context of resurrection (ii) the context of eschatology and (iii) the context of narrative. These must be dealt with briefly in turn.

(i) All the New Testament writers believed that Jesus had really died, and had been raised by God from the dead. Recent study of the resurrection belief of the New Testament writers has strongly emphasised the fact that the resurrection traditions of the different writers are the appropriate points of culmination for their particular versions of the gospel (e.g. Evans 1970). 'Resurrection' it appears is not a naked fact to be interpreted, but an alleged divine intervention bearing from the first a theoretical content. And this content is most conspicuously eschatological. The resurrected one is seen as a *future* deliverer. One of the earliest descriptions of a Christian group reports how they 'turned to God from idols, to serve a living and true God, and to wait for his Son from heaven, whom he raised from the dead, Jesus who delivers us from the wrath to come' (1 Thess. 1:10). Resurrection, moreover, for all the writers either entails, or is followed by, exaltation; and the exaltation of Christ is the final determination of his position viz-à-viz mankind (that is, his Lordship) and the real beginning of a new order of things. This sequence is significant. For although Jesus appears to have been condemned on the charge of having entertained regal political ambitions ('the King of the Jews'; Mk. 15:2 and 26), it seems that the early church itself did not connect the theme of sacrifice with that of kingship. We may see this in, for example, the Book of Revelation, where both the sacrificial death of 'the Lamb' is emphasised (5:6ff; 7:14; 12:11) and also the kingship of Christ (17:14; 19:16) but the Lamb is never spoken of as a king *before* being slain. Kingship is always seen eschatologically (see Lohse 1976: 95—6). Moreover, in one of the Gospels where the kingship of Christ plays an especially prominant role, the gospel of Matthew, it has been argued that the death of Christ is not viewed as a sacrifice (See Gerhardsson 1974: 25—35). Thus the themes of Kingship and of sacrifice are generally separated, the one who is slain not being regarded as king before the sacrifice.

(ii) This fact helps to emphasise the importance for all the sacrificial language of the New Testament of the context of eschatology. It is, of course, true that the eschatological beliefs of the New Testament writers and of their sources are still more diverse than their resurrection beliefs. Moreover, within the period covered by the writing and compilation of the New Testament documents there is evidence of change and development, the precise course of which it is exceptionally difficult to chart. However all writers agree that the *basileia* or Kingdom is the central theme of the public proclamation of Jesus. That this term is so much less prominent in, for example, the writings of Paul provides strong evidence of the essential reliability of the Gospel traditions on this point, and also of the sheer fact of the impact made by the resurrection faith in the primitive community. The major point however on which both Jesus and Paul are agreed is that 'now is the day of salvation' (2 Cor. 6:2—cf. Kümmel 1974: 142). Both are persuaded of the imminence of the eschatological consummation of salvation. Although in his understanding of the means of salvation, Paul reflects the altered situation of the primitive community after the death and resurrection, convinced, as he is, of the presence of the end-time in the resurrection, nonetheless the pull of the future continues to be evident in Paul's thought. Salvation for him continues to be 'in hope'. The present reality of salvation, through the justification of the sinner or through his baptism, conceived of as dying with Christ, and through participation in the Lord's supper, conceived of as sharing in his body, is always qualified by the expectation of a divine goal which will complete and confirm what is here and now only partial. Both the sacrificial death of Christ, and still more the Lord's Supper (which is a 'proclamation of the Lord's death until he comes', 1 Cor. 11:26) is invariably contextualised by eschatology.

(iii) The sequential stamp imposed by eschatology on the beliefs of the early Christian communities is one element in the fundamentally narrative character of the Christian gospel. The long apologia ascribed to Stephen, opening with the words, 'The God of glory appeared to our father Abraham . . .' (Acts 7:2), is in the form of a narrative explaining precisely the significance of the coming of the 'Righteous One' and his murder, in the context of a persistent misapprehension about the significance of the temple for Israel's worship. The narrative is, in effect, a reconstruction of the significant moments in Israel's history; so, also, is the parable of the vineyard owner and his tenants in Mark 12, which culminates in the murder of the son and heir. The new identity of the Christian community is demonstrated in its capacity to tell a different story about God's dealings with Israel from that told by the Jews who remained faithful to their traditions. The explanatory key to the story is, naturally, Jesus, who is now risen and exalted, and whose coming is awaited.

Here, however, we observe a peculiar feature of the narrative context of the sacrificial language of the New Testament. This total story of God's dealings with humanity contains within itself the story of a particular person. There are, thus, two stories, one within the other, but each requiring the other. Neither is, or could be, independent of the other. Both are, ultimately, stories whose theme is the salvation of man; but whereas the first, total story is, to put it crudely, 'about' God himself, the second is 'about' Jesus. The two stories have separate foci; and it has been suggested more than once that they provide alternative bases for the development and nurture of Christian piety.[6] How they are related, or, more precisely, the acute difficulty of successfully relating them, constitutes the major point of this present paper.

The first, total story has to do with a general picture of world history, and God's covenant with Israel and through Israel with all mankind. The second story is more highly domestic and familiar, having to do with one man, Jesus of Nazareth. This story, however, tells of his crucifixion, a repulsive death indicative of his rejection by, and separation from, the holy people of Israel. That event could not stand on its own as the mere factual circumstance necessarily preceding resurrection and exaltation. It required contextualisation, either as the typical fate of a prophet ('it cannot be that a prophet should perish out of Jerusalem'; Lk. 13:33), or as the death of a martyr similar to the Maccabeean martyrs, or as the death of an innocent victim. In the case of the latter two the prehistory of the slain one and of his manner of death is an essential element in the story. To know that a person was a martyr or an innocent victim one must be in possession of the circumstantial details leading up to his death. Thus, one of the essential functions of the gospels is to provide a narrative context in which Christ's true meaning of his sacrificial death might emerge. A capacity to recall the whole story is therefore a necessary part of the proper recollection of his death. That the death had a particular time and place is what the words 'who, on the same night that he was betrayed, took bread . . .' strongly emphasise. The Calvary deliverance has to be remembered in a story.[7]

The three aspects of the context in which it was affirmed that Jesus's death was a true sacrifice lead us to the following summary conclusion: *Christian speech about the death of Jesus is invariably part of a sequence which rehearses his life, death, resurrection and exaltation, and which sets before the hearer the present demand and future promise of the Kingdom.* These are constituent elements of the new world of meaning in which the slaying of Jesus is denominated a sacrifice.

III

The central section of this paper is concerned with what the New Testament has to say about sacrifice, in respect of the death of Christ. This enquiry entails, of course, immersing oneself in one aspect of the very mainspring of Christian belief and devotion. In dealing with one aspect, however, it is extremely difficult to avoid, and not entirely desirable that one should avoid, entangling oneself in all the other major, and related aspects of the same religious world of meaning. The limitations imposed by the writing of a single contribution on this theme have necessitated also abandoning any intention of writing a review of the New Testament data on sacrifice; this has been done competently in a number of encyclopaedia articles, to which the reader is referred (See esp. Wendland 1960: 1647—51; Brown 1978: 415—36).

What perhaps a non-specialist in New Testament studies can usefully offer is a theory about the structure of the New Testament data. Much of the specialist literature has concerned itself with primarily historical questions. How did Jesus view his own death? What was actually said and meant at the last supper? What Old Testament texts lie behind the writers' sacrificial language? Important though these questions are, they are not the only ones which may properly be asked of the New Testament. For if the Christian Church, in the highly active, twenty centuries of its intellectual history, was either unable or unwilling to propound a definitive theory in explanation of the death of Christ, it may not unreasonably be asked, what problem, or problems, in the New Testament inhibited such a development. And, to apply the same question to the question of sacrifice, it may well be asked, what basic problem, or problems, arise when the term 'sacrifice' is taken into a Christian world of meaning, and new content is given to it, related to the new orientation of the believer and his new patterns of worship. Such questions are not wholly historical, although historical considerations are certainly relevant in any attempt to answer them. What is also to the point, and what I shall be at pains to develop, is a theory which tries to offer an explanation for the fact that

the New Testament writers write so elusively on the subject; but a
theory which also accounts for why subsequent generations of Christians
have found that elusiveness both frustrating (in respect of their urge
towards the systematization of their beliefs) and profound (in respect
of its capacity to elucidate the human situation).

What follows will deal with the New Testament documents in
three sections, devoted to (i) the Jesus traditions, (ii) the theology of
Paul and (iii) sacrifice in the other New Testament writings. That no
review of the documents is being offered will be evident in the cavalier
lumping together in the third section of such diverse documents as
Hebrews, 1 Peter and the Johannine writings. The justification for this
procedure, however, lies in the argument about the basic problem of
'sacrifice'; this problem, I shall try to show, emerges in the first section
on the Jesus traditions, comes to open expression in the Pauline
writings, and is merely illustrated and confirmed in the rest of the
New Testament. The problem is thus bequeathed unresolved to subsequent Christian history; and the final section of this essay will briefly
suggest why Christians continue to find wrestling with the same
problem far from being a stultifying exercise in reconciling the unre-
concilable.

(i) The Jesus traditions

A most obvious feature of the New Testament communities is the way
in which the language of the Jewish cult—sacrifice, offering, temple
and priesthood—rapidly came to be redeployed. In due course members
of the early Christian groups ceased to participate in the worship of
the Jewish synagogues. If the stages and pace of this process of separation are a matter of obscure conjecture, the outcome is clear. Christians,
by virtue of being Christians, ceased to attach any constructive religious
significance to the Jewish sacrificial cult; and the reason for this
astonishing fact lies not in any direct attack by Jesus on the sacrificial
system, but in the refocussing of religious attention, and thus of the
religious world of meaning, a development by means of which the
early Christian communities reached a consciousness of their own
independent identity.

This process of refocussing starts, of course, with Jesus himself,
and contains as *part* of its outcome the focussing of attention upon
Jesus himself. But the important point to grasp is that, from the first
(that is, from the traditions which can with some historical reliability
be ascribed to Jesus himself), there are two elements in the process—
one element which concerns teaching about God, his nature and his

act, and a second which is associated with Jesus and the significance of his life's work. The argument of this essay is that these two elements, present in the Jesus traditions themselves, are acutely developed by Paul and reflected in the rest of the New Testament, thus constituting the major thrust of the theological bequest of the documents to subsequent Christian history.

This bequest, social anthropologists will note, is literary and intellectual in character, and not, in the first instance, a matter of ritual. That the teaching about sacrifice led, in due course, to the ritual expression of the Christian eucharist is absolutely plain from the history of Christianity; but what is also plain is that Christianity itself, at the Reformation, threw up as a major development *of its own tradition* a sharp criticism of the apparent independence of cult and rite from the basic moral and spiritual orientation of the believer. At the very least, therefore, students of the Christian religion have to recognise the importance of the study of texts laying great emphasis upon the inward disposition of man before God ('truth in the inward parts', Ps. 51:6 in Coverdale's translation). From the first, it seems, Christian groups engaged in the close study and interpretation of the Old Testament; what absorbed their attention was, then, primarily texts about sacrifice, rather than sacrifices themselves.

Full weight, therefore, has to be given to the fact that Jesus himself was a teacher and interpreter of texts. Although he had apparently little or no formal training, and perhaps belonged to an informal tradition of charismatic prophets at odds with the Pharisaic establishment (So Vermes 1973a: 58—60), nonetheless the subject-matter of Jesus' teaching is recognisably in the tradition of that offered by contemporary Jewish students of scripture. He was, and was recognised as, a teacher of the Jewish law; and as such his message fundamentally concerned God, his nature and activity. Both themes are contained in the Markan summary of Jesus preaching, 'The time is fulfilled, and the kingdom of God is at hand; repent and believe in the gospel' (Mk 1:15). Teaching about the nature of God is implicit in the demand for repentance, since God is seen as one who accepts and welcomes the sinner who repents, and restores him to full familial status (hence the address of 'Father'); and reference to the activity of God is implicit in the eschatological concept of the fulfilment of the times in the proclamation of the gospel by Jesus. The 'at hand'-ness of the kingdom of God is the result of *God's* activity; attention is, accordingly, to be focussed on what he has done. The crowds at Capernaum ask with amazement what new thing is Jesus' teaching and healing (Mk 1:27); the Nazareth synagogue are told that Isaiah's prophecy of one who will preach good news to the poor has now been fulfilled (Lk. 4-18 and 21). Even without an explicit attack on the temple sacrifice, attention is being drawn away from it.[8] Jesus goes no further than accepting, as part of his teaching about God, the prophetic critique of sacrificial religion (Mt. 9:13 and 12:7, citing Hos. 6:6; and Mk 12:33 referring to 1 Sam. 15:22). This reinforces his demand for purity of intention as a condition of genuine repentance, and his preference for the sinner who honestly recognises his sin over the one convinced of his own ritual purity in God's sight.

In order to identify the full impact of this first element in the Jesus traditions on sacrifice, we have to recognise that there takes place in Jesus' teaching a revival and reapplication of a long tradition of concern for the universal character of Israel's mission. In the prophets, the glory of God is shown to the whole world (Zech. 2:17), as a result of which the Gentiles gather at Jerusalem and sit down to a heavenly banquet (Isa. 25:6—9). In the Jesus traditions, a Roman centurion is praised for his faith in Jesus, and a saying is added to the story:

> I tell you, many will come from the east and west and sit at table with Abraham, Isaac, and Jacob in the kingdom of heaven, while the sons of the kingdom will be thrown into outer darkness; there men will weep and gnash their teeth (Mt. 8:11—12, cf Lk. 13:28—30).

By those who 'come from east and west' unquestionably is meant the Gentiles; and although there were considerable problems to be surmounted before the gospel could be preached among Jews and Gentiles equally, the idea that at the last day there would be table fellowship between Jew and Gentile could not but have a profound effect on the practice of the Jewish cult. As we shall see, the table fellowship of the eucharistic cult, itself seen as a foretaste of the Messianic banquet, was based on the concept of a new covenant with all men. 'In the message of Jesus, the universalism of grace takes the place of national particularism' (Jeremias 1972:247). This universalism is a reworking of traditional doctrines about God, his nature and activity; it is of profound significance for the terms on which God and man are said to be related, and thus indirectly for the Jewish practice of sacrifice.

Closely connected with this first element in the teaching of Jesus himself is the second, namely the significance given, both by Jesus and by others, to himself and his activity. That this second element likewise entails a shift of focus is apparent in the Matthean statement, 'I tell you, something greater than the temple is here' (Mt. 12:16). The christo-

logical direction of this shift of focus becomes fully explicit in the
statement of Mark 10:45 ('the Son of Man also came not to be served
but to serve, and to give his life as a ransom for many'), and the narratives of the Lord's supper. Both of these have provoked a considerable
scholarly dispute over issues on which a non-specialist naturally hesi-
tates to take sides; and what follows can only be said to be one of the
possible ways of interpreting them. It seems reasonable to argue that
the term ransom (*lutron*) expresses a selfless devotion to the whole
people which would shrink from no extremity of cost.[9] The phrase
obviously undergoes further development until it is found in the
theology of a Hellenistic community as an interpretation of the sal-
vatory power of the death of the mediator between God and man ('the
man Jesus Christ, who gave himself as a ransom for all', 1 Tim. 2:5f).
Its significance in the Gospel tradition, however, is its capacity to
interpret both Jesus' action—especially his devotion to the poor—
and the rejection and opposition which Jesus encountered, and which
culminated in his death. Only if in reality we can trace the marks of
selfless self-dedication does such a statement carry conviction.

The most important Jesus tradition of the same type is found in his
words at the last meal with his disciples. These exist in four differing
accounts (1 Cor. 11:23—25; Mk 14:22—25; Mt. 26:26—29; and
Lk. 22:15—20); John, astonishingly, has no account of the last supper
and only a few verses contain a direct allusion to a eucharistic meal
(6:51b—53). The differences between these narratives and the difficulty of their interpretation make the reconstruction of what was said,
done and intended a highly conjectural affair. Some argue that Jesus
himself interpreted his death as a representative sacrifice on behalf of
all men (Jeremias 1966; 1972: 288—90). Others find no sacrificial
meaning in Jesus' language, seeing the words merely as a statement
that Jesus' death initiates a covenant which his entire activity and
teaching have set in motion (So e.g. Kümmel 1974: 90—2). Fortun-
ately it is unnecessary to decide these disputed questions here. For our
purposes it is quite sufficient to make an examination of the earliest
certain account of what Jesus was thought to have said which had a
bearing on the practice of the Church—that is, the account of Paul
in 1 Corinthians 11.

This turns out to be remarkable enough. Paul's description of the
last supper is not set in a section either of reminiscence or of liturgical
instruction, but rather in the middle of a piece of acutely practical
exhortation about the divisions which have occurred at their meetings
as a church (vv. 18—19). The richer ones, it appears, had been humili-
ating the poorer by eating and drinking conspicuously before the

Lord's supper, and by not sharing the available food (vv. 20—22). At the end of the chapter his instruction is that when they come together to eat they are to wait for one another, lest they 'come together to be condemned' (v. 34) (Cf. Bartchy 1979). In between these highly particular social directions he recounts, as though it constituted a final argument against the behaviour of the Corinthian congregation, the tradition he receives from the Lord, how 'on the night he was betrayed, took bread' etc. (vv. 23—26).

Here we must recall the significance of Jesus' teaching about table fellowship with Gentiles noted above, of his open practice of table fellowship with tax collectors and sinners (Mk 2:15—17; Lk. 7:36—50; Lk. 19:7) and of the tradition of interpreting his whole life's work as that of service at table ('For which is the greater, one who sits at table, or one who serves . . . But I am among you as one that serves', Lk. 22: 27; cf. the washing of the disciples' feet: Jn 13:3—16). This is tantamount to the paradox of presenting the Messiah serving at the Messiah's own meal (So Jeremias 1966: 205). Similarly in his instruction of the Corinthian Church, Paul wants his hearers to be in no doubt what participation in the body of Christ means. A man who eats and drinks 'without discerning the body' (v. 29), and thus incurs a judgement which starts to take effect even here and now, is one who does not perceive that the memorial of Christ's death entails the intimate social fellowship of a common meal.

Even though we are unable to proceed with any certainty to speak of Jesus' own intention in relation to the repetition of his last meal with the disciples, it is significant that both the 'ransom' saying of Mark 10:45 and the Pauline account of the last supper coincide in highlighting a particular aspect of Jesus' actual practice. The abstract and virtually undecidable question of whether some *previous* concept of sacrifice has influenced Jesus' own thought about his own death is no longer of major significance. For what is emerging is consciousness of a new focal point in the religious life of man, according to which a sacrifice of ultimate significance has taken place in the death of a man who had acted in a certain way.

There are thus two elements in the Jesus traditions: one concerns the nature of God and his contemporary act seen especially in its eschatological significance, as focussing attention away from the old sacrificial cult; the other concerns the particular quality of Jesus' own life and the narrative of his way of death, rehearsed as a memorial of a new covenantal relationship between God and man. Both of these elements are, as we shall see, taken up by Paul and other New Testament writers, and pass firmly into the central Christian tradition.

(ii) *The theology of Paul*

In Romans we have what is acknowledged to be the most sophisticated treatise upon 'the gospel', for which Paul considers himself to have been set apart (1:1), and of which he is not ashamed (1:16). No one reading chapters 1—3 of that letter can fail to note the position which the 'wrath of God' occupies in his explanation. This wrath or retribution he sees as now falling upon the 'godless wickedness' of men (1:18); it is visited not merely on those who grossly follow shameful passions; it falls also on the few, who dishonour God by breaking the law (2:23f.). God has no favourites (2:11); the whole world is exposed to his judgement (3:19).

This is the immediate context in which the gospel has to be set; hence the words 'but now' (*nuni de*, 3:19) with which Paul's firs statement about the significance of Jesus Christ:

> But now the righteousness of God has been manifested apart from law, although the law and the prophets bear witness to it, the righteousness of God through faith in Jesus Christ for all who believe. For there is no distinction: since all have sinned and fall short of the glory of God, they are justified by his grace as a gift, through the redemption which is in Christ Jesus, whom God put forward as an expiation by his blood, to be received by faith. This was to show God's righteousness . . . (Rom. 3:21—25. R.S.V.)

The context shows how clearly Paul associates the death of Christ and judgement for sin. He returns to the same theme in chapter 5:

> While we were yet helpless, at the right time Christ died for the ungodly . . . God shows his love for us in that while we were yet sinners Christ died for us. Since, therefore, we are now justified by his blood, much more shall we be saved by him from the wrath of God. (5:6—9).

Here the wrath of God is spoken of as poured out in a future judgement when those who would otherwise expect to be condemned will not be condemned.

I have emphasised the theme of sin, wrath and judgement because it shows how thoroughly Paul sets his language about Christ's death in an ethical context. The sins which he details in chapters 1 and 2 are various—idolatry (1:23), homosexual practices (for which Jews had a special loathing, 1:26—27), and a long list of vices (including covetousness, malice, envy, murder, deceit, insolence, disobedience to parents, lovelessness and pitilessness, among others, vv. 28—31) which was conventional in the Hellenistic world and of which other examples appear in the New Testament.[10] It is from the divine judgement on such conduct that God has provided an expiatory sacrifice (*hilasterion*); this is his 'means of dealing with sin' (So Barrett 1971: 77—8). As a result of this sacrifice sinners are justified (by faith), and delivered from future wrath.

Now it cannot escape attention that Paul is proposing at the very least a moral paradox. It is God himself who is the judge; it is God who sets forth Christ to be the expiatory agency, through his death; and it is God from whose wrath man is saved. It appears that God is offering himself as a sacrifice in the person of his (innocent) son. But Paul never explicitly says so. What he does say, later in Romans, is that

> God has done what the law, weakened by the flesh, could not do: sending his own Son in the likeness of sinful flesh and for sin, he condemned sin in the flesh in order that the just requirement of the law might be fulfilled in us, who walk not according to the flesh but according to the spirit. (Rom. 8:3—4)

The justification of man is, at the same time, a condemnation of, or passing judgement against, *katakrima*, sin. Or in 2 Corinthians, we find Paul saying that

> God was in Christ reconciling the world to himself . . . For our sake he made him to be sin who knew no sin, so that in him we might become the righteousness of God. (2 Cor. 5:19 and 21)

Or in Galatians

> Christ redeemed us from the curse of the law, having become a curse for us—for it is written, 'Cursed be every one who hangs on a tree'—that in Christ Jesus the blessing of Abraham might come upon the Gentiles. (Gal. 3:13—14)

In each of these statements the death of Christ is the God-ordained means of rectifying the situation between God and man, which preserves the full seriousness of the human condition.

The movement of this theological position towards a morally monstrous saga in which God engineers human salvation by means of the ritual slaughter of his own innocent son—what one might call the remythologisation of atonement—is powered by Paul's determination to hold on to his basic sense of 'the wages of sin' and its capacity to tyrannise over human life. Although such a saga might be deduced from the references Paul makes to the atoning efficacy of

Christ's death, nowhere does he baldly rehearse it; and there is a reason for this reluctance which lies in another essential part of his theology, his teaching about Christ's self-offering.

The key to understanding why this is integral to Paul's theology lies in seeing the same two elements as we have identified in the Jesus traditions at work in the heart of his concept of the focus of his religious world of meaning. In all the passages we have referred to above *God* has been the subject of the action of sending, setting forth, condemning sin, reconciling man and so forth. But Paul also regards *Christ* as himself the focus, frequently coupling God and Christ in such formulae as 'in God through our Lord Jesus Christ' (Rom. 5:11) and 'to God in Christ Jesus' (Rom. 6:11, cf. Rom. 8:39), or focussing on Christ alone. For Paul, of course, preaching the cross of Christ is the essential task of the apostle (1 Cor. 1:17—25). Christ is the foundation of all Christian living (1 Cor. 3:11); Christian bodies are the members of Christ (1 Cor. 6:15); the whole congregation is the body of Christ (1 Cor. 12:27); to be 'in Christ' is Paul's most striking way of referring to the new quality of life of Christian discipleship in the light of the resurrection (1 Cor. 15:22). There is, therefore, little likelihood that Paul's view of Christ's death would be exclusively God-focussed. And so it turns out. In a passage which is conceivably a pre-Pauline hymn (and which significantly constitutes an attempt to hold together the two foci), Paul speaks of Jesus as in essence like God, but ready to surrender this likeness to God and to assume the human form of existence; furthermore 'he humbled himself, and became obedient unto death, even death on a cross' (Phil. 2:8). The fact that the whole passage is introduced as the paradigm of a life of unselfishness and humility indicates the point of focus upon Christ. Here is one, the events of whose life provide the horizons for and aims of the disciples' lives. Looking to the interests of the other (Phil. 2:4) is one aim of a life styled on the events of Jesus' life. There are numerous other indications of the same basic feature. Christ is 'the last Adam' and is a life-giving spirit (1 Cor. 15:45). Baptism into Christ is a union with him in his death, with a view to full participation in his resurrection (Rom. 6:3—11). The Christian life is seen no longer as obedience to the law, but as a crucifixion with Christ, 'who loved me and gave himself for me' (Gal. 2:2; cf. Gal. 6:14 and Phil. 3:10). Jesus, the resurrected and exalted one, now lives to intercede with God on the sinner's behalf, and nothing will separate the Christian from the love of Christ (Rom. 8:33—5, also speaking of 'the love of God in Christ Jesus our Lord', v 39). The 'meekness and gentleness' of Christ are invoked (2 Cor. 10:1) and also his love for his neighbour (Rom. 15:2—3).

The explicit application of this focus upon Christ becomes clear in the letter to the Ephesians (which contains Pauline elements, if not written by Paul himself).

> Be imitators of God, as beloved children. And walk in love, as Christ loved us and gave himself up for us, a fragrant offering and sacrifice to God (Eph. 5:1f).

If the argument of this paper has carried conviction at all, the temptation to regard the words 'a fragrant offering and sacrifice to God' as a metaphor ought to have evaporated. Certainly the word 'fragrant' is metaphorical in this context, referring to incense offerings.[11] But in the Christian world of meaning, the death of Christ is the climax of his offering of himself in love for others. It is a sacrifice whose nature cannot be appreciated apart from a rehearsal of the events of Christ's life, for without such a narrative there would be no knowledge of the love which motivated him. It is, moreover, a sacrifice which Christians, in utter conformity to Christ (they are, after all, to 'take the shape of Christ', Gal. 4:19, NEB), are to offer, presenting their own bodies as a holy and acceptable sacrifice to God, 'which is your spiritual worship' (Rom. 12:1). In the Christian world of meaning these sacrifices are no more metaphorical than is Christ's. From other standpoints such sacrifices are, no doubt, 'spiritualized', in as much as the fruit of the sacrifice is, in the broad sense, spiritual and ethical (see Rom. 12:3—21). But it is quite correct to draw attention to the acute ambiguity of the concept of 'spiritualization', and to the plain fact that Paul has in mind the presentation of the Christian's *body* to God, and thus not a non-material entity (as does Daly 1978: 6—8). From the Christian standpoint, his life is the festal celebration of self-offering, inaugurated by the sacrifice of Christ (cf. 1 Cor. 5:6, where Christian living after the sacrifice of Christ, the Passover lamb, is spoken of as the celebration of a festival).

In summary of our examination of Paul, the following may be said: The sacrifice of Christ has to be looked at in two ways. First, it has to be seen as the act of God in the desperate context of human sin, of which God is the wrathful judge. By means of that death, man's relationship with God is changed; he may be 'justified by faith', and God's judicial sentence against him may be altered. Secondly, the sacrifice of Christ has to be looked at as the climactic act of a life of self-giving, an act with a voluntary and purposive intention, whose quality is taken to be paradigmatic for all future human life. This bi-focal character of what is said about the death of Christ has a number of immediate and long-term consequences, such as the chronically unsystematisable character of Paul's thought and the motivation for the further reflection which produced, in due course, the Christian doctrine of the Trinity.

(iii)   *Sacrifice in the other New Testament writings*

Since this is not a review of the New Testament data on the subject of sacrifice, but rather an attempt to provide a theoretical structure for such a review, it will be sufficient merely to note the same bi-focal characteristic in the other New Testament books. In the epistle to the Hebrews the subject of sacrifice lies at the centre of the author's profound attempt to come polemically to grips with the ritual of the Day of Atonement—a cult of which he seems to have had mainly book knowledge. The author, in line with the tradition we have observed, is concerned with texts about sacrifice. Basing his argument on the conception of an eternal and perfect high-priesthood, he interprets the death of Christ as that of the self-offering of a holy, blameless and unstained high-priest (7:26f). The two foci are here brought together; on the one hand, the act of God in appointing one to make purification for sin (1:3), and on the other the character and act of one who is able 'to sympathise with our weaknesses, but one who in every respect has been tempted as we are, yet without sinning' (4:15).

What the author of Hebrews brings out, however, with special force—be means of a remarkable combination of eschatology with the theology of expiatory sacrifice—is the eternal dimension of the act done in time. Christ, he urges, has entered heaven itself, of which the Old Testament tent or tabernacle is but a copy. His sacrifice is 'once for all at the end of the age' (9:26), and by it 'he has perfected for all time those who are consecrated' (10:14). The fact that, as it appears, Christ *continually* intercedes with his blood in the presence of God on behalf of sinners (Heb. 9:24) provides the essential key to the readiness of the early church to speak of the eucharistic worship of the church as a sacrifice. The memorial of the 'new covenant in my blood' (1 Cor. 11:25) is the rehearsal of the foundation act of the new age, the sacrifice of Christ. If that sacrifice is being eternally pleaded on behalf of sinners by the exalted Christ in the heavens, it is but a short step to say that the prayer of the Christian body at the eucharist joined with that of Christ, its head, is itself the offering of a sacrifice. [12]

The same feature characterises the theological thought of the writer of 1 Peter. Here the shedding of the precious blood of Christ 'like that of a lamb without blemish or spot' (1:19), is spoken of as having been predestined by God, as the means of ransom, from before the foundation of the world (1:20). But at the same time, the story of Christ is explicitly rehearsed (with conscious echoing of the Suffering Servant of Isaiah 53) as an example of the patient suffering of injuries.[13]

> To this you have been called, because Christ also suffered for you, leaving you an example, that you should follow in his steps. He committed no sin; no guile was found on his lips. When he was reviled, he did not revile in return; when he suffered, he did not threaten; but he trusted to him who judges justly. He himself bore our sins in his body on the tree, that we might die to sin and live to righteousness. By his wounds you have been healed (2:21—24).

The writer of 1 Peter is, like Paul, ready to speak of the sacrifice of Christian living. The whole Christian community is a 'holy priesthood' offering 'spiritual sacrifices' through Jesus Christ to God. The mediatorial role of Christ in this sacrificial act again provides a warning against viewing the Christian sacrifice metaphorically.

Finally we must refer briefly to the Johannine writings. It is here that we find the most well-known of the sacrificial texts of the New Testament, the statement attributed to John the Baptist, 'Behold, the Lamb of God, who takes away the sin of the world!' Despite its familiarity, however, the background of this sentence is very obscure. On the one hand it seems that John is elsewhere concerned to emphasise the coincidence of the Passover sacrifice and the death of Jesus (Jn 19:14 and 31); (compare the use of hyssop, 19:29, and the preservation of Jesus' bones unbroken, 19:36, recalling Passover regulations, Exod. 12:22 and 46). On the other hand, the death of the passover lamb was not thought to take away sin. It seems possible that John has either combined for himself, or used a source which combined, a paschal and an atonement motif. One possibility is the so-called Akedah, or sacrifice of Isaac, told in narrative form in Genesis 22 and given a richer interpretation in early rabbinic Judaism. According to this interpretation, whose origins it is impossible for us to date with any precision, the sacrifice is spoken of as if it had actually taken place, Isaac being represented as a mature man voluntarily acquiescing in it. Furthermore this sacrifice is regarded as the expiatory sacrifice *par excellence*, which subsequent sacrifices are designed to recall.[14] Even if the rabbinic interpretation of the Akedah is not pre-Christian, it is certainly contemporary with early Christianity and may be taken at least to illustrate the thought-world in which the voluntary death of a mature man may be spoken of as having the atoning power of an expiatory sacrifice. The same background may be invoked for that development whereby the cult of the new Christian community was held to entail a 'remembering' of the archetypal sacrifice of Christ.

The dual focus, as we have analysed it in the other strands of the New Testament, is powerfully present here also. For in the text of the Genesis narrative we find Abraham's assurance to Isaac that 'God will provide himself a lamb for the burnt offering, by son' (Gen. 22:8); and in the rabbinic interpretation the one spoken of as 'the lamb of the burnt offering', namely Isaac himself, gives himself up voluntarily. Similarly, in the gospel of John, Jesus is the lamb *of God*, that is, God himself provides the Lamb (or, to use a parallel expression of John's, he 'gives his only Son . . . so that the world might be saved through him', Jn 3:16 and 17); and, on the other hand, Jesus gives himself, laying down his own life of his own accord (Jn 10:18), and giving his flesh like bread for the life of the world (Jn 6:51)). Moreover, the life of the Christian is explicitly spoken of as a reduplication of that quality of love found in Christ's own self-sacrifice. 'Greater love has no man than this, that a man lay down his life for his friends. You are my friends if you do what I command you' (Jn 15:14).

IV

It remains to enquire into the significance of this bi-focal view. The first answer to this question is that it introduces a polar tension into the Christian understanding of the nature of God, and thus into the Christian understanding of man. Of course, the Christian tradition is that there is one God; the tension, therefore, exists *within* God as so conceived. But the Christian *account* of God is in two stories not one: a story of power, transcendence and judgement—and a story of weakness, immanence and forgiveness. The sacrifice, which is the death of Christ, is at once a powerful condemnation of sin, and a victory over the forces of evil, and also a supreme act of humble self-identification with the powerless. From this bi-focal view springs the enormous resilience of Christian faith and its capacity for adaptation to vastly different circumstances; from it similarly springs the ambivalence in its attitude to worldly power, whether that of its own hierarchy or of that of the state.

But we will have missed what I dare to think is the perennially fascinating quality of this Christian understanding of sacrifice if we fail to penetrate a little further into the *moral* significance of this dual, or bi-focal view. Paul, if the argument above is correct, is neither saying that Christ is simply the final and completely efficacious sin-offering, put forward by God to appease his own wrath against human sinfulness; nor is he simply saying that Christ is the paradigm of the highest moral life conceivable, that of humble, self-giving service for others. Rather he wants to say, if this is not too elusive a way of putting it, that the moral world is such that God's judgement on man is passed, *sub specie crucis*. This condition does not entail in any degree minimising the horror of the moral degradation of humanity, from the foulest excesses of the gas-chambers and torture rooms, to the subtle and pervasive corruptions of self-deception. The proclamation that man is responsible and will answer for his deeds is irremovable from the Judaeo-Christian tradition. And yet, at the same time, the dimension of tragedy in human existence is neither denied nor circumvented, a tragedy for which the only conceivable human response is a deep compassion, which voluntarily burdens itself with the fate of another or of others.

To treat the death of Christ as a morally edifying tale is to trivialise it. That this was done quite early in the history of Christian interpretation is true. Professor MacKinnon (1974: 129) rightly speaks of

the emergence of an apologetic style which seeks to make the intolerable bearable, even edifying, which seeks also to eliminate the element of unfathomable mystery by the attempt to move beyond tragedy.

The argument here can perhaps be illustrated by reference to *Measure for Measure*, surely one of Shakespeare's most theologically perceptive plays.[15] Here we are presented with a commentary on two styles of judgement upon the human condition, both of which are found to be, by themselves, inadequate. On the other hand, the strict, retributive justice of an Angelo, who without fear or favour would visit the full ferocity of the law upon each offender, is constantly shown to be lacking in common humanity; more subtly, on the other hand, the conventional piety of an Isabella, who explicitly invokes the divine pity as an example of human conduct when faced with wrong-doing ('He that might the vantage best have took/Found out the remedy'), is also seen as helpless in the face of an acute, and tragic alternative. With both styles of response to the test set his subjects by the Duke on his departure, the play shows itself thoroughly dissatisfied.

From the moment that the Duke disappears to observe his subjects' response to his absence, the audience is built up stage by stage towards a 'final judgement', a scene of revelation in which both Angelo and Isabella are brought to plead for grace, but in very different terms; Angelo for the grace of an immediate death, and Isabella for Angelo's life. The Duke's devices achieve, thus, a reversal in both the initial

styles of judgement. Angelo sees himself, in the light of his own retributive standards, as wholly disgraced ('I crave death more willingly
than mercy'), desirous only of a quick end to his shame. Isabella, also,
is brought to a reversal. Her piety is no longer the conventional
religiosity of the ritually pure, and her plea for Angelo's life is not an
appeal for 'cheap grace'; it is a powerful, contra-natural petition based
on co-humanity in suffering. It is the crucial moment of the play,
skilfully heightened for the audience by their knowledge that she still
thinks that Claudio, her brother, has been cynically executed by
Angelo in contravention of their bargain. At this moment with stunning
poignance, Shakespeare will have Isabella recognise the element of
justice in Claudio's fate, and yet also, by an act of sheer grace, speak
as though the crime had not occurred.

> Most bounteous sir,
> Look, if it please you, on this man condemn'd,
> As if my brother lived: I partly think
> A due sincerity govern'd his deeds
> Till he did look on me; since it is so,
> Let him not die. My brother had but justice,
> In that he did the thing for which he died:
> For Angelo,
> His act did not o'ertake his bad intent,
> And must be buried but as an intent
> That perished by the way.

The feebleness of the excuse is infinitely less impressive than the
contradictory bringing together of an act of intercession against retributive justice ('An Angelo for Claudio, death for death'), made by one
who herself recognizes the appropriateness of retribution.

Measure for Measure is not a precise analogue of divine judgement;
the role of the Duke is sufficiently ambiguous and compromised to
dispel any such impression. Nonetheless the play is a profound, and
perhaps conscious, exploration of the theme of grace,[16] and the movement of the play consists in the revision and expansion of the moral
judgement of the audience. It is a puzzling tale, whose lack of moral
homogeneity has a disturbing way of revealing more about the critic's
own assumptions and moral attitudes than is usual. I would argue that
the reason for this is its insight at once into the bi-focal character of the
Christian understanding of sacrifice, as outlined above, and also its
capacity to create resonance with, and thus to illuminate, the ultimately mysterious moral situation of man, caught between responsibility and compassion.

NOTES

1. As 'for example' does Masure 1944: esp. 35, 78—80.

2. Dr James Woodburn, Senior Lecturer in Anthropology at the London School of Economics, made clear in oral contributions to the discussion that certain hunting and gathering societies (such as the Hadza) had no sacrificial rituals.

3. Thus the Council of Trent: 'One . . . and the same is the victim, one and the same is He who now offers by the ministry of His priests and who then offered Himself on the Cross, the difference is only in the manner of offering'; session XXII, c.2. Latin text in Denzinger 1967: 408—9.

4. Cf. the same problem arising in respect of 'worship'. Smart 1972: 3–5.

5. It should be noted that the sentence 'to sacrifice one's children *to* one's career' uses a different preposition from 'to sacrifice one's career *for* one's children. Sacrifices can be made *to* someone (usually a deity, hence metaphorically 'to one's career', making it a 'god') and *for* or *on behalf of* someone. The ambiguity of the second sentence lies in the absence of any statement about the intended direction of the sacrifice.

6. See, for example, Stephan 1960: 3—4, on the 'extensive' and 'intensive' movement of faith.

7. See Rogerson's observations on the recital of the Exodus deliverance, in his contribution to this volume.

8. For unqualified references to Jewish sacrifices see Mk 1:44; Mt. 5:23—4; Mt 23:18—9.

9. So Barrett 1972: 20—2, arguing against the interpretation which sees the background of this saying in the Suffering Servant picture of Isa 53. For the opposite view, see Jeremias 1972: 286—8.

10. At Rom. 13:13; 1 Cor. 5:10—11, 6:9—10; 2 Cor. 12:20—21; Gal. 5:19—21; Eph. 4:13, 5:3—5; Col. 3:5, 8; 1 Tim. 1:9—10; 2 Tim. 3:2—5.

11. Paul uses it in 2 Cor. 2:14—16 and Phil. 4:18 of the preaching of the gospel ('we are of the aroma of Christ') and of the gifts of the Philippians to himself ('a fragrant offering, a sacrifice acceptable and pleasing to God').

12. It is a further step taken by a Latin writer of the early third century, when to the bishop is attributed the power of 'high-priesthood' to make atonement before God and to offer the gifts of the church. Once the prayer of the *bishop* is identified as a sacrificial act, there opens the possibility of viewing the church's public celebration of the eucharist as the sacrifice *par excellence*, if necessary apart from the self-offering in Christ of the whole community in its dedication to its practical tasks. See Daly 1978: 133.

13. The early Christian communities increasingly used the Suffering Servant of God of Isa. 53 as a prediction of the sufferings of Christ and to reinforce the teaching concerning their representative significance—see also Acts 8:32; Hebs 9:28; 1 Clement 16:3—14 and Barnabas 5:2. That Jesus himself so read and understood Isa. 53 is argued strongly by J. Jeremias (1972: 289—91). Apart, however, from Lk 22:37 and Mt. 8:17 there is an absence of firm indications, and this must count against supposing that such an interpretation formed an important or central part of Jesus' own teaching.

14. For a brief outline, see Daly 1978: 47—9; and Maier 1972: 118—21. A fuller treatment may be found in Daly 1977. See Dr Hayward's appendix below.

15. It is not necessary to argue that Shakespeare was a 'consciously and distinctively Christian' dramatist, or that the play is a 'Christian parable', in order to support the assertion that *Measure for Measure* is theologically perceptive. As R. M. Frye (1963: 272) has argued, 'The overwhelming concern of his drama is with those areas which are universally human'. But this by no means precludes the fact that, in *Measure for Measure*, we find a remarkable treatment of a central Christian theme. What is 'distinctively Christian' and what is 'ethically perceptive' are not simple alternatives. Further discussion in Knight 1930; Leavis 1942; Battenhouse 1946; Hunter 1965.

16. 'Grace is grace, despite of all controversy', Lucio in Act 1, scene 2.

APPENDIX: THE AQEDAH

Robert Hayward

According to Rabbinic interpretations of Genesis 22—preserved in Talmud, Targum, and Midrash—Isaac, the Only and beloved son of Abraham was bound and offered as a sacrifice on Mount Moriah, where the Temple was later to be built.[1] He was thirty-seven years old, and Abraham had told him that he was to be the victim, the sacrificial lamb.[2] Isaac willingly accepted this. He and Abraham went 'with a perfect heart', and with careful attention to the *halakhah* offered an umblemished sacrifice.[3] Although Isaac was not killed, it was accounted 'as if' he had been, and the sacrifice was in every respect perfect.[4] Some sources speak of his shedding a quantity of his blood, and of his ashes: but others say nothing of these things.[5]

A ram lamb, specially created on the first Sabbath eve, was offered in Isaac's place.[6] By this lamb he was redeemed. Isaac's sacrifice is held to validate all future lamb offerings, in particular the *Tamid*: and his one perfect oblation was understood as making effectual all Temple sacrifices.[7] Thus God is asked to remember the Binding of Isaac, and thereby to answer the prayers of his descendants, to forgive their sins, and to rescue them from trouble.[8] This sacrifice is the setting for a covenant between God and Isaac, which issues in benefit for Israel and blessing for the Gentiles.[9]

From the second century AD until the present, Jews have celebrated Isaac's Binding on New Year's Day.[10] The pre-Christian Book of Jubilees, however, linked Isaac's sacrifice to Passover, a tradition which is endorsed by the Targums.[11] These last state that the 'memorials' of Creation, God's covenant with Abraham, Isaac's birth, Exodus, and Messianic Redemption are celebrated at Passover along with the Binding of Isaac. Thus Isaac, 'the lamb of the burnt offering', is put into the same theological continuum as the Passover lamb. By a lamb was Isaac redeemed, and by a lamb was Israel redeemed—at Passover.[12]

This complex of traditions is known as the Aqedah (Binding) of Isaac. The individual elements which make up the complex probably emerged and developed at different times, and should be examined and dated separately.[13] As Vermes and le Déaut have shown, most of these elements are attested by writings of the first century AD; but neither these writings, nor the Targums, speak of Isaac's blood.[14] This fact tells against the opinion that the Aqedah as a whole originated in the second century AD as a Jewish counterblast to Christian doctrines of the Atonement, in which Jesus' blood is essential.[15]

Jubilees fixes the Aqedah at Passover time on the Temple Mount: Abraham and Isaac appear as confronting and defeating the powers of evil.[16] Philo sees the event as a real and perfect sacrifice;[17] IV Maccabees agrees with Philo, and depicts Isaac as the archetypal martyr, whose offering is purificatory and propitiatory.[18] Josephus remarks that Isaac was an adult who joyfully offered himself,[19] and Pseudo-Philo's *Liber Antiquitatum Biblicarum* relates Isaac to the sacrificial lambs of the Temple cult: his offering will issue in blessing for all men.[20] The essentials of the Aqedah, therefore, are as old as the first century AD, and certain features, for example its connection with Passover, are pre-Christian.[21]

Although there is not complete agreement on the matter, some scholars argue that the New Testament writers knew and used Aqedah traditions: there is every likelihood that these scholars are correct.[22] It is becoming clearer that St. John, for example, was familiar with Targumic traditions;[23] and his description of Jesus as 'the lamb of God who takes away the sins of the world' is more easily explained by the Aqedah than by other Jewish prototypes.[24] Such an explanation clearly merits serious consideration.

Finally, just as Isaac's unique offering was 'remembered' in the daily sacrifices of lambs in the Temple, so Jesus' unique oblation is recalled in the Eucharistic sacrifice. The Aqedah has been suggested as a paradigm for this[25], and it would make excellent sense. St. Paul compares the Eucharist directly with pagan and Jewish sacrifices;[26] and from the time of I Clement and the Didache onwards the Eucharist is invariably called a sacrifice.[27] But what may be particularly significant is that the Roman Liturgy, renowned in antiquity for its conservatism, alludes to Abraham's offering of Isaac as a type of the *Eucharistic* sacrifice, and this in a prayer bearing the marks of Jewish tradition. Thus the priest asks God to accept the Eucharist

as Thou didst accept the gifts of thy righteous servant Abel, and the sacrifice of our Patriarch Abraham, and the holy sacrifice, the spotless victim, which thy high priest Melchizedek offered unto thee.[28]

NOTES

1. The Palestinian Targums (hereafter PT) to Gen 22:10 call Abraham and Isaac Unique Ones. They are thus like Adam before he left Eden, who was Unique on earth as God is Unique in heaven (Targum Neofiti to Gen 3:22), and like Israel (Targum Pseudo-Jonathan to Num 23:24). Jews manifest God's Uniqueness in reciting *Shema^c* and in dying as martyrs like Rabbi Akiba, who expired uttering the ONE of *Shema^c* (b. Berakhoth 61b; yer Ber 9:5, 14b). For Mount Moriah as the site of the Temple, see II Chron 3:1; Josephus *Antiquities* I.226; PT to Gen 22:14; Gen Rabbah 55:7.

2. The whole Rabbinic tradition agrees on his age; e.g., Gen Rabbah 56:8; Ps-Jon to Gen 22:1. For his identification with the lamb, see Fragment Targum, Neofiti and its glosses to Gen 22:8, and cf. Vermes 1973b: 196—7.

3. See PT to Gen 22:10; Gen Rabbah 56:8. A 'perfect heart' means complete moral, religious and intellectual integrity in loving God: see Sifre Deut 32; b. Ber 54a; Philo, *de Abrahamo* 198. For the *halakhah*, see Gen Rabbah 56: 8; b. Shabbath 54a; Ps-Jon to Gen 22:3.

4. See particularly PT to Gen 22:10.

5. For Isaac's blood, see Mekhilta of Rabbi Ishmael (ed. J. Z. Lauterbach, Philadelphia, 1933), *Pisha* 7, lines 78—79; *Beshallah* 4, lines 84—91; Mekhilta of R. Simeon b. Yohai (ed. J. N. Epstein, Jerusalem 1955), p. 4. For his ashes, see Sifra (ed. J. H. Weiss, Wien, 1862), p. 102c; yer Ta' anith 65a; Gen Rabbah 49:11; Fragment Targum ed. B. Walton (SS. Biblia Polyglotta, London, 1657) and Neofiti to Gen 22:14. See also below, n. 14.

6. Ps-Jon to Gen 22:13; b. Pesahim 54a; m. Avoth 5:6. The tradition is probably attested by I Peter 1:19—20; Rev 13:8; see le Déaut 1961.

7. See Ps-Jon to Lev 9:2—3; Neofiti and glosses to Lev 22:27; Lev Rabbah 2:11; le Déaut 1963 171—4; Vermes 1973b: 208—11.

8. See PT to Gen 22:14; Gen Rabbah 56:10.

9. See Ps-Jon and Fragment Targum (ed. M. Ginsburger, Berlin, 1899) to Lev 26:42; Ecclus 44:22; Ps-Jon to Gen 22:16 —18.

10. See Musaf service for Rosh ha-Shanah; b. Rosh ha-Shanah 16a; Lev Rabbah 29:9; Lévi 1912.

11. See Jubilees 17:15—16, 18:3—19, 49:1; PT to Exod 12:42.

12. See le Déaut 1963: 131—211.

13. See Vermes 1970. Developments of the Aqedah in post-Talmudic times are discussed in Spiegel 1967.

14. For what follows, see Vermes 1973b; 193—204; le Déaut 1963: 179—201. P. R. Davies (1979: 59) defines Aqedah as 'an actually accomplished sacrifice in which blood was shed'. But the Targums to Torah speak of Aqedah without ever mentioning Isaac's blood: see Neofiti and Fragmentary Targum to Gen 22:14.

15. See Geiger 1872; Davies 1979.

16. See Jubilees 18:13, and above, n.l. Mastema, prince of evil, initiates the Aqedah and is frustrated, 17: 16; 18: 12; cf. Gen Rabbah 56:5.

17. See *de Abrahamo* 168—77; *de Migratione* 142; *Quod Deus immutabilis sit* 4, where Isaac is called a 'thank-offering' (*charistērion*).

18. See IV Macc 6: 28—9, 13: 12, 16: 20, 17: 22. The Targums imply this by calling Isaac a Unique One; see above, n.l.

19. See *Antiquities* I: 227, where he is twenty-five, and cf. variant reading in Gen Rabbah 56:8. All speak of Isaac's willingness; Philo, *de Abrahamo* 172; PT to Gen 22:10; IV Macc 13: 12; Josephus, *Antiquities* I: 232; *Liber Antiquitatum Biblicarum* (LAB) 32: 2—4.

20. See LAB 32:3, where Isaac announces: 'My blessedness shall be upon all men, for there shall be none other'.

21. For a different view, see Davies & Chilton (1978), Davies (1979: 67) argues that Aqedah was originally tied to New Year. But this seems strange if, as he believes, the Aqedah originated as a polemic against Atonement wrought by Jesus *at Passover*.

22. For a selection of these scholars, see Davies 1979: 61, and note his disagreements with them.

23. See Hayward 1979: 25—7.

24. See Professor Sykes's remarks above, and Vermes 1973: 223—5.

25. See Vermes 1973: 225—7. Note that Aqedah and Eucharist share covenant associations, and that Passover and covenant were linked in pre-Christian times: see Wisdom 18: 9, and Jaubert 1963: 356 n.14, 358.

26. I Cor 10:16—21.

27. I Clement 36: 1; Didache 14:2; see further Couratin 1969.

28. In the bible, Abel is not called righteous, nor is Melchizedek high priest, but they are so described in Targum: see le Déaut 1962: 222—9.

RITUAL IN PERFORMANCE AND INTERPRETATION: THE MASS IN A CONVENT SETTING

Suzanne Campbell-Jones

'There is nothing more important than the Mass. The Mass means everything to us. It was the ultimate sacrifice. Our lives are consecrated to Him. Our lives are given to Him and He gave his for everyone.' These are the words of a nun talking about a central ritual in the Catholic Church, a woman in her sixties looking back on a lifetime of dedication within a religious institute.

I

In the period 1969 to 1974, I was engaged in anthropological fieldwork among two congregations of working nuns.[1] During this study, I encountered various interpretations of the Mass, the most extreme of which could almost be placed outside Catholicism, within the commensality of the Protestant interpretation of the Eucharist. Here I am concerned with these interpretations of the meaning of the 'ultimate sacrifice' and its symbolic representation in the Mass.

Some justification for bringing the Mass into a discussion of sacrifice is needed. Although the Roman Catholic usage of 'sacrifice' to refer to the Mass has become part of the English language, the rites are far removed from the ritual killings which most of the essays in this collection deal with. Edmund Leach, in his essay on 'the logic of sacrifice' (1976: 92) comments that 'sacrifice in Christianity appears only in vicarious symbolic form as a reference to mythology', which seems to imply that the Mass is not the same kind of activity as the ritual killing with which he is primarily concerned. Nor does the Mass seem at first sight to contain what Beattie regards as the central feature of sacrifice: the killing, immolation, of a living victim.

Beattie is following Evans-Pritchard's definition of Nuer sacrifice, which excludes libations of food and drink, but which significantly includes rites in which a wild cucumber is substituted for a sacrificial ox (1956: 197). In the case of the Mass, the Catholic belief that the bread and wine used in the Mass are transformed to acquire the status of a real sacrificial victim provides at least as real a victim as the wild cucumber is for the Nuer. This is illustrated by Sister Mary, who sits closer to the tabernacle because she believes in the 'real presence' of Jesus Christ; any remaining consecrated bread is preserved in the tabernacle. Sister Mary believes in the magical transformation of the humble bread and wine. But if you questioned her, she would deny that her beliefs are magical. She would say that it is a mystery. Mysteries are articles of faith. They are not to be questioned. They are part of the *credo* which, as Hubert and Mauss point out (1964: 28), provides an 'unshakeable confidence in the automatic result of sacrfice'. In their classic study of the nature of sacrifice, these French anthropologists commented (1964: 101) 'Religious ideas, because they are believed, exist; they exist objectively, as social facts.' Sister Mary's belief that in the Mass Jesus Christ is actually present as a real sacrificial victim is as important a fact as any ritual action we may observe.

In order to understand ritual from an anthrological point of view, both the actions and the statements about them must be accepted as valid *data*. In examining the Mass as sacrifice, we pay attention not only to what is done, but also to what is said about it. One of the primary qualities of any ritual is its communicability. In listening to the participants we can learn about the context of belief and there lies much of our explanation. We can acknowledge the traditional validations of beliefs. We can even accept the attempts of theologians schooled in divinity and Church history to add an intellectual gloss to the magical and mystical elements of Church rite. Every congregation of nuns has its own specialist interpreter. But when Sister Mary tells you that the closer she sits to the tabernacle the closer she sits to God, the anthropologist must be interested in why that should be.

When we take the actions and the words of the Mass together, we find that the ceremony comprises a re-enactment of the Christian story of the god who came to earth as a man and then sacrificed himself to provide a perpetual link, a channel of grace between mankind and god. In his contribution to this volume Sykes has shown how the symbols of sacrifice are central to this story. The Mass can thus be compared with the Dogon sacrifices described by Mme Dieterlen (1976), which re-act a primordial mythical sacrifice, which in turn is central to the Dogon understanding of the world.

In his discussion of sacrifice, Leach presents a model by means of which we can begin to decode religious rituals, revealing the relationship between the 'world of physical experience and the other world of metaphysical imagination'. In this model, 'the purpose of religious performance is to provide a bridge, or channel of communication, through which the power of the gods may be made available to otherwise impotent men' (Leach 1976: 82). I shall show that the Mass provides such a bridge or channel for the nuns, who derive spiritual strength from the ritual.

Leach also speaks of the way in which 'the continuous flow of normal secular time' is broken by the insertion of 'intervals of liminal, sacred non-time' (1976: 34). Another anthropologist, Victor Turner puts the same point more positively:

> In the life of most communities, ancient and modern, there appear to be interludes in historical time, periods of 'timeless' time, that are devoted to the celebration of certain basic postulates of human existence, biological and cultural. This 'moment in and out of time' (to quote T. S. Eliot) is the moment when ritual is being performed. In most known societies it is a time for meditation upon, or veneration of, the transcendental . . . (1968: 5)

He points out that the appropriate behaviour in such interludes is formalized, even rigidly so, and symbolic, to the effect that gestures, words and objects used, together with myths and doctrines which explain them, convey more than their superficial meanings. Turner suggests that the repetitiveness of rituals instil beliefs and values, and that rituals have real, purposive effects on the lives of the people performing them (1968: 6). All this clearly applies to the Mass, in which the nuns cut themselves off from their normal working lives to participate in what they believe to be 'one and the same sacrifice' as the offering by Jesus Christ of himself on the cross nearly two thousand years ago.

The ceremony of the Mass, like all rituals, is conducted as a drama, in a stage setting with actors and audience. My first task is to describe this 'significant space' as Leach calls it, and to sketch in the major elements and participants. Those closer to the faith than I will recognise only the simplest references to the complexity of procedures. I make little reference, for example, to the various degrees of solemnity with which the Mass can be celebrated, and none to the calendrical variations in the Catholic Church's liturgical celebrations. Further, I am not concerned with the variety of explanations and interpretations of the Mass which can be found in theological and other cicles outside the convents.

I have selected three contrasting settings to illustrate three main types among the numerous interpretations and social groupings which exist in the congregations I studied. All three could be found in England in 1970, but the first more rightly represents the past: a rigidly conservative convent barely touched by the reforms that overtook the Catholic Church in the early 1960s. The second setting is a contemporary progressive convent of the same congregation. The third is a traditional Franciscan congregation which felt little need to change. These three settings highlight different aspects of the Mass, which correspond with particular sacrificial themes: the offering of a gift and the symbol of death in the first setting; the communion meal in the second; and consecration and making contact with the deity in the third.[2]

II

There was, in the North of England, a large convent, custom-built in the 1890s for a congregation of nuns who taught middle-class girls in an attached boarding school. The spatial and temporal dimensions of the convent are expressive of both social requirements and religious beliefs. It has high walls, windows well above peering height, a massive metal-studded front door and a slim wooden side door for tradespeople and for lay sisters (those engaged in the menial work of the convent). The boarding school was enclosed to the south, and the sisters' living quarters to the north of the main hall. The hall itself had a very high ceiling and, opposite the main door of the convent, three stone arches, the middle one leading to a chapel entrance—a doorway flanked by stone recesses for holy water. Thus the chapel became at once an inner sanctum and the focal point for the architecture of the convent.

Not only architecture: colours, too, played a part in the preparation of the faithful for the full glory of the chapel. The ceiling of the outer hallway was painted pale blue in contrast to the long corridors leading away on either side which were uniformly dark red or dark green, relieved only by the dark castellated architraves of doorways. The sisters moved from the earthy, secular colours of the convent corridors into the azure haze of the chapel. There the colours were white, pale pink, pale blue; and high above the vault was the focal point—impaled on a huge red cross, the nailed figure of the suffering Christ. Add to this sensuous imagery, the smell of incense and the gentle flickering of candles, lush floral tributes and maybe a dark veiled sister, arms outstretched, swaying before the representations of the crucifixion agony in the 'stations of the cross'. This was the setting for the daily re-enactment of the nuns' belief in their God's sacrifice for them. On the huge crucifix the suffering Christ was their heavenly spouse, the sacrificial victim, the saviour to whom the daily prayers and the whole life of the nuns were dedicated.

The nun's understanding of the Mass depends on its context of a dedicated life. Sykes has pointed out that the efficacy of Christ's sacrifice depends not simply on the moment of Calvary but on the Bible story of the man who dedicated his whole life to mankind. The nuns say, 'our lives are consecrated to him. Our lives are given to him as he gave his for everyone'. Sister John, entering the convent in the 1920s, as a young girl, was preparing for a lifetime of renunication and self-sacrifice. In his discussion of the economics of sacrifice, Raymond Firth concludes that sacrifice is the giving of oneself or part of oneself, through the offering of a surrogate. He comments, 'in the ideology of the symbolic equivalent of things—the greatest surrogate of all is the sacrifice of mind and heart, the abnegation of individual judgement and desire in favour of devotion to more general moral ends.' (Firth 1963: 21). We can apply this to the nuns' understanding of their self-offering. A girl entering the old conservative convent left behind her clothes, her name, her legal rights, her talents and her freedom of action. Total self-abnegation was expressed in the interpretation of the vows. The vow of obedience, for example, bound the nun to obey any command or demand of her superior, and to guard her behaviour at every moment of the day. To leave a tap running would merit a penance. In the morning the nuns were spreadeagled on the floor of the chapel in 'profound genuflection', in the evenings they stooped to kiss the dust of the floor of their cells reminding themselves that they were as nothing —dust. These symbolic actions reinforced the images of death and the destruction of the self which were repeated in the sacrifice of the Mass.

A series of dramatic rituals separated a new novice from the world outside and confirmed her in her new identity as a member of a community of consecrated virgins. The vows of poverty, chastity and obedience bound her to the congregation and gave her a special relationship, the Bride of Christ. She now stood between the carnal secular world and the Other-world—an intercessor, a witness, for believers in the Other-world of saints, spirits and God himself. She was in effect a member of a spiritual élite. Familes were, in general, happy for their daughters to enter the convent; their pride might well be tinged with relief that someone close to them was now closer to God. Someone whose life of prayer might be answered favourably. No sacrifice is made without some expectation of a good return.

The nuns who entered the Gothic chapel were themselves part of the drama of sacrifice. They were in a liminal position between this world and the Other-world. But they were not the most intimate with the source of power which was believed to emit from the Other-world: there was yet another intermediary—the priest. In the traditional world order of Tridentine Catholicism the priest was as much feared as respected. The groups of nuns, under their mother superior, saw their relationship to their father/priest as one of dependency, awe and respect. God the Father was also held in awe: he had a 'fearful majesty'. At the Mass, the priest repeated for the congregation the words and actions of his sacred prototype, Jesus Christ—God the Son. The nuns were 'brides of Christ': it was to him that they offered their consecrated virginity. The relationships between deity, priest and congregation was extremely complex. To engage in the sacrifice of the Mass, both priest and congregation underwent various purifactory rituals and put on special clothes. All the participants would recently have confessed their sins and received absolution from a priest; and they would have prepared themselves for Mass and the eucharist with fasting and prayer. The choir nuns took an additional veil over their heads for Mass, and the priest's vestments included an amice over the shoulders, the long white alb, the cinture, the stole and the chasuble. While the priest's proper domain was the sanctuary, the nuns were restricted to the nave of the chapel, separated from the altar—the focal point for action—by the altar rails. This concern for the maintenance of boundary, and the attention given to purity and pollution, is an expression of the social divisions (class hierarchy and status differentiation) of Church and convent. The only nun allowed beyond the altar rails was the Sacristan. She was always a lay sister and held her office for life. She was generally held in special affection by the the other sisters. It was her primary duty to keep a lamp burning before the tabernacle. She was allowed to touch the chalice, paten, palls and corporals but not after they had been used in the ceremony of the Mass. They had to be washed by a cleric in major orders and the water of consecration poured into a sacrarium or thrown on a fire. The extreme caution with which ritual objects, including consecrated oil and water, were treated reflects not only their concern with the boundary between this world and the next, but with Church hierarchy; the humble nun must not contaminate articles handled by the consecrated priest.[3]

The Gothic chapel was designed so that the nuns sat in rank order in prie-dieu before the altar rails. There were three steps up to the main altar which was set behind pillars carrying three arches, the recurring multiple of three being a reference to the Holy Trinity. The tabernacle could be seen through the central arch. In the ceremony of the Mass, bread (the host, from *hostia*, a sacrificial victim) and wine are taken before the altar, and consecrated with solemn invocations by the priest. On solemn occasions, burning incense is shaken over the offerings and about the altar. At the moment of consecration, the bread and wine are mysteriously changed into the actual flesh and blood of Christ, the Son of God. Catholics are instructed to believe that it is not just Christ's body substance which appears under the guise of bread and wine, but his whole personality, renewing his sacrifice on the Cross (Denzinger 1967: 386; cf. 389 can. 2). The Council of Trent declared that this is 'the same Christ contained and immolated in an unbloody manner, who, on the altar of the Cross, offered himself once in a bloody manner' (Latin text in Denzinger 1967: 408). The doctrine of the 'real presence' adds considerably to the mystery and magic of the Eucharistic sacrifice. Hubert and Mauss contribute to our understanding of this ritual. They find a consistent relationship between god and victim, priest and victim, such that it is a god already formed that both acts and suffers in the sacrifice:

> Nor is the divinity of the victim limited to the mythological sacrifice; it also appears in the actual sacrifice which corresponds to it. Once the myth has taken shape it reacts upon the rite from which it sprang and is realised in it. Thus the sacrifice of the god is not merely the subject of a good mythological story. Whatever changes the personality of the god may have undergone ... it is still the god who undergoes the sacrifice, he is not a mere character in it. (Hubert and Mauss 1964: 88)

The relationship between the Christian myth of the God who sacrificed his son to redeem mankind is not, either in the terms of the Council of Trent, or in the beliefs of the nuns in their Gothic chapel, a 'vicarious symbolic form only' as Leach suggests. In the daily Mass the repetition and reiteration of God's sacrifice, which involved according to the story the horrific and bloody sacrifice of a man, acts to ward off the chaos and evil of this-world with help from the divine power of the Other-world. The Mass contains the central piacular idea of substitution—son of God for mankind, bread and wine for son of God. Thus the redemptive sacrifice of the god is perpetuated throughout time. It opens up a channel (grace) between sacred and profane worlds through the meditation of a victim which is, in the course of the myth and the ceremony, destroyed. In the context of the Gothic chapel, the nun comes close to the immanence of her God but not too close. She takes a little comfort and a lot of spiritual strength from her participation in the sacrifice. In providing for a liminal priest to perform the sacrifice in the liminal zone before the altar, she has moreover, 'provided a bridge between the world of the gods and the world of men across which the potency of the gods can flow' (Leach 1976: 14). The nun at Mass was witness to a drama. A drama played out in a representation of cosmological space: the high altar, the shrine representing the Other-world; the area before the altar, liminal space; the place for the congregation, this World. The action takes place in cosmological time, in which mythological events are replayed for the present.

In the course of this dramatic ceremony, the nun approached the altar rail, provided she was in a state of ritual purity, and took the bread (host) in her mouth. The priest alone could drink the wine. The taking of the host was both a commemorative act, in remembrance of the Last Supper, and 'food for our souls'. Great emphasis was placed on the need for purity for the reception of the Eucharist. To receive unworthily is sacrilege, and this thought provides the Mass with a strong normative influence on the lives of the nuns. It is only through the atoning sacrifice of Christ, in which the nuns shared, that anyone could dare to approach so sacred a meal and receive from it an abundance of spiritual strength: they explained that the 'sanctifying grace' received through communion kept one's soul alive and helped one to keep free from sin.[4]

Since the sacrificial ritual depended on the priest's correct performance of the consecration rite, the priest held a position of immense power. He alone could open and close the channels of life——renewing grace which flow from the sacraments. As one of the sisters said, 'If the priest was not there then that bread would not change into the body of Christ. The priest has to be there. It's a tremendous power isn't it? The Church hierarchy held an unrivalled position as guardian and sole introit to the supernatural.

The setting of the rigidly conservative convent was one of clearly defined and hierarchical boundaries. God is awesome and remote. He was approached through a priestly intermediary, who alone had access to the sacred objects of the sanctuary, and who was himself an authoritative figure. The nuns in turn were in a position to intercede for the world at large, by sharing in the offering of the priest and the sacrifice of Christ. In this hierarchical setting, sacrifice was primarily understood as the death of a divine victim, who alone could atone for the outrage of disobedience to so awesome a God. The nuns' sharing in this sacrifice was understood as a sharing in death, through the self-abnegation in their lives. Through this propitiatory sacrifice, man and God are brought together in communion.

III

Tridentine Catholicism relied on the 'closed' nature of its belief system and on discrete social groups for its plausibility. Changes in the last fifty years threatened the plausibility of these religious definitions of reality.[5] The sacrificial drama in the Gothic chapel could only belong to the old order. It was an age when an ordered hierarchy of officials discharged their duties within the demands of the religious Rule. It was an age of obedience and rank, of self-sacrifice and abnegation. The congregation had been founded not only with religious aims but also to educate Catholic girls. By the 1950s, the demand for private schooling had dropped: not only was the value of this secondary objective questioned, it was becoming an economic straitjacket. The bureaucracy's response was even greater conformity. Instrumental values tended to become terminal values. There was pressure for change, for a change of goals, of government, of life-style. Then the Second Vatican Council insisted on all religious congregations submitting themselves to a rigorous questioning of values and goals. This congregation of teaching nuns was in crisis. There was a fundamental incompatibility between their traditional beliefs, their Rule, their founder's precepts, the demands of religious life and the radical Catholicism of the 1960s.

The teaching congregation has now sold all its large schools and its nuns pursue a number of different secondary vocations, including nursing, social work and looking after the aged. They live in ordinary houses, often in run-down city areas. The doors of their convents look like any other door in the street. There are no purpose-built chapels. I was talking to a jolly middle-aged nun in a comfortabe sitting room. She was wearing comfortable clothes, a brown skirt and cardigan, sensible shoes, a pretty blouse. One of her fellow sisters came in wearing a plain blue dress, lace-up shoes and a small veil perched on the back of her head. Both had known years of the full religious habit, the old system of permissions, silences, enclosure. Now they laughed and told me that the Church is alive in the world and that the work they do is out there, in the living Church. Tonight they will celebrate Mass in the house. Have a meal, then the Mass, then a discussion. 'The priest uses the desk over there for his things. We don't mind where, it gets a bit crowded if there are more than four of us.' The relationship with the priest was crucial. He had to be 'understanding', the Bishop had to by 'sympathetic'. In the old order, the nuns accepted the authority of the Church and its representatives without question. Now an individual might travel many miles to find a confessor-priest to suit her, and in the case of disagreement with a local bishop the organization simply moved into another diocese. In this way, the power of the hierarchical Church had been modified.

In the Mass, the power of consecration still rests in the priest, but he is now willing to share the ceremony with his congregation and bring the audience into the action, expressed in their drinking the communion wine and passing the chalice from hand to hand. The 'real' presence' is experienced through people in their relationship with one another around the communion table. The supernatural force of that presence is felt as the cup is passed from hand to hand. One sister said, 'I don't think the priests realise what an impact that makes on people. It hits you like anything when you go into Mass and the chalice is passed round. You don't lose anything of your belief that it is the real presence.' Another confirmed this view by saying, 'I can't explain, but it gives me a wonderful feeling, the sharing and the receiving the precious blood . . . it does something to me.' Whereas before communion involved a relationship between each nun and the awesome God, now communion also expressed inter-relationships within the community.

Barriers and the boundaries they marked have been weakened, both the barriers between the nun and the supernatural and those between the nun and the secular world. Breaking down the latter barrier makes her feel more vulnerable. But the full burden of that position is deflected from the individual nun into the group. The nuns emphasize the ritual *sharing* of the eucharist. Sister Therese said, 'a few years ago, the receiving of communion was something intensely personal . . . now I see it in a different way, apart from the individual relationship and the contact with Christ, I can see it is historically based on a meal and it's a social event.' Another sister always told her catechetics class that the covenant with God was made over a meal, including the unleavened bread. 'The idea that the bread is nourishment, and in this case it nourishes us to love one another. The Eucharist is just like family meals at home, the bread nourishes spiritual life. But the blood and body are more difficult to grasp. A body to a child is dead and lifeless. ' I asked whether she thought of the Eucharist in this way. She did. Moreover she took only the bread at communion.

Those nuns whose belief in the 'real presence' was unshaken, shared modern egalitarian relationships with their priest which echoed their relationship with a close, friendly divinity in touch with humanity. It is a move to a more mature relationship in which the father is no longer to be feared. Freudian interpretations would draw attention to the importance sisters attached to taking the bread and 'feeding ourselves.' Sister Anne tried to explain, 'You see as a child I had always a great fear of the retaliation of God—I think this lies at the heart of the relationships with God, whether he is an awesome and wrathful figure or whether he is kind and forgiving. When personal responsibility suddenly became the keynote I suddenly felt infantile.' This sister spent three years in religious crisis until she found an answer for herself, 'Man is the image of God's thought. God is an essence. It is in the nature of God to be self-sufficient, eternal, and that is expressed in the human personality. When man commits a sin or destroys himself he is commiting evil because he is destroying the image of God. It is up to us to preserve God's image.' Sister Anne was one of a group of sisters who lived by the credo: 'We are all one body because we are all partakers of that one bread.' It is expressed by Norman Brown (1966: 167): 'The transubstantiation is the unification; is in the eating. By eating we become his body; eating makes it so.'

The progressive sisters used the symbolism of the Eucharist to express their sense of community. There had always been a sense in which the white circle of bread symbolised the body of the faithful. But now God himself had become a small-group member and the nuns could talk to God directly and without intermediaries. There have always been channels open to the faithful which give them direct access to heaven, channels which were exemplified by the mystics' face-to-face communion with their God (exemplified in the lives of St Therese of Avila, St John of the Cross). There is no secularisation of beliefs among the progressive nuns, rather a shift in interpretation to make allowance for changes in organisational patterns and forms of lifestyle. I would not want to take a determinist stance in explaining this change, rather to hint at an internal dialect between the believer, her beliefs and her social life.[6] When the sisters say that they put less stress on the sacrificial aspects of the Eucharist and more on the covenant they are talking about the divine drama. Their own evidence shows them to be just as dependent on the original myth, that God sacrificed his son for them and that his covenant was to leave open a channel of grace for the redemption of mankind. To this extent at least, the Mass remains a purificatory ritual and a piacular sacrifice.

The emphasis of the progressive nuns on commensality brings to mind Robertson Smith's communion theory of sacrifice, in which the victim is a totemic symbol of a clan or group. According to this theory in various ways the sacrificial victim is, at the moment of destruction, identified with the deity. This is clearly illustrated in the sacrificial words of the Shilluk divine king: 'The flesh of this animal is as my flesh, and its blood is the same as my blood.' (Evans-Pritchard 1956: 280n.) These words are comparable to those of the Christian 'King of Heaven' which are repeated in the Mass. There is a totemic significance in communion with the gods: the sharing of one flesh clearly delineates a ritual group. In the Christian story, the god takes on human form, he bleeds and dies. The act of consecration recreates this humanity under the form of bread and wine. In the ritual partaking of flesh and blood, the identification between man and god is complete, and the partici- pating group is united in a blood covenant of immense power.

The modern nuns can cite early precedents for finding God in a small group around a living-room table. In the first three centuries of the Church's history, not only was the Mass primarily an act of com- munity but the bread used in the ceremony was a staple foodstuff. The historian Nicholas Lash (1968: 100) gives evidence that the ordinary Christian in the early Church had a most concrete image of the Mass, comprising blessing, sharing and consuming food and drink. It was only later, during the Middle Ages, when the Church made more of its power as a mediator and the Latin language created an ever-widening barrier, that ordinary people became excluded—audience rather than actors.

The two settings we have examined so far have provided distinct, though not contradictory, interpretations of the Mass, emphasizing the propitiatory death of the victim in the first case and the community meal in the second. In accordance with the ambiguity that is to be found in symbols in most cultural and social contexts,[7] the Mass is sufficiently ambiguous to allow alternative interpretations to co-exist. If we can agree with Raymond Firth (1973: 419) that the Eucharist contains a statement about power and the source of power, we can readily under- stand how the complex of sybols contained in that ritual can represent a hierarchical power structure in one context and a loosely-structured group in another. 'Religion legitimates social institutions by bestowing upon them an ultimately valid ontological status, that is, by locating them within a sacred and cosmic frame of reference.' (Berger 1969: 33.) The ritual provides a 'sacred canopy' of symbols making up a world picture appropriate to the structure or organization of the celebrants, whether thay are a practising ritualized group like the convent of nuns, or a disparate collection of laity recognising their common membership of the wide Church.

IV

We come now to the third social setting, that of the Franciscan con- gregation, modelled on the Franciscan Order, which has its origins in a reaction against the hierarchical exclusiveness of the Church during the Middle Ages.

The congregation of Franciscan missionary sisters were distinguished to me as being one of the most 'conservative' congregations in England.

They still lived, in the 1970s, in large convents or out on the missions, in the full habit, enclosure and silence of traditional Tridentine Catholicism which placed God out of reach. They retained the full panoply of secondary rituals, such as the rosary and the Stations of the Cross, and yet they could reach their God at any hour, in any place, and he was a friendly, loving God. The particular legitimation of authority in this congregation was through the unique relationship of its founder, Saint Francis, with God and with the Church. The Mass, for these Franciscan sisters, was still a great sacrificial banquet held in a chapel loaded with sensuous imagery, colours and sacred icons. Saint Francis was a mystic who claimed direct contact with the supernatural through 'visitations'. His message was simple: reform through individual example by love and virtue. The Church, well aware that it could not afford a rival who threatened to bypass its channels of communication with the supernatural, had two choices, to outlaw or to institutionalize. By recognising the special qualities of the saint, the rebel could operate within the legal bounds of Church authority. The Testament which Saint Francis left as the ideal blueprint for his followers was a powerful document 'divinely inspired' on the occasion of his vigil on Mount Verna when he was imprinted with the 'stigmata'. The stigmata was an impressive symbol; with it he became the living image of Christ crucified. Canonisation brought this highly dangerous man within the orbit of Church authority. The personal qualities of the saint became organizational values for the Church and for the religious orders based on this Rule and Testament. To become a friar, a man should give up everything. His path through life would be one of poverty, healing and preaching to the poor.

For the Franciscan sisters three closely woven themes—self-sacrifice, the sacrifice of Christ and the sacrifices of St Francis—dominated their interpretation of the Mass. The Mother-General said, 'We have now many girls coming forward for formation. You know young people really want to give up everything to be a nun or priest. They really have to make a sacrifice and to feel that they are giving up their all. They can do so many things these days—be lay missionaries, work in slums, teach, nurse—without being a nun. The religious life has to have something different about it.' She actually found the idea of 'God in humanity' absurd. She said that God is to be loved for himself. In giving themselves wholly for the love of God, they are making up for all the people who do not believe he exists. In these Franciscan convents, as in the conservative teaching convent first described, from their liminal position the nuns offer themselves for the guilt and sins of mankind.

Evans-Pritchard (1956: 281), writing about Nuer cattle sacrifice, said:

> When the Nuer give their cattle in sacrifice they are very much, and in a very intimate way, giving part of themselves. What they surrender are living creatures, gifts more expressive of the self and with closer resemblance to it than inanimate things, and these living creatures are the most precious of their possessions, so much so that they can be said to participate in them to the point of identification.

The Mass is seen as a sacrifice because it re-affirms the nuns' own total self-offering. The Novice Mistress explained:

> The Mass is a sacrifice. Christ is sacrificed, offering his sacrifice to his heavenly Father, pleading for us, for our needs. When we go to the Blessed Sacrament we are coming into the presence of Christ in the form of bread. The priest in valid orders has made that possible. It is an enormous mystery . . . With faith it is the most marvellous miracle that God could make himself present all the time since Christ's own coming on earth through his death and resurrection. So we are nearer to God when we are in the chapel and actually in prayer. When we visit the Blessed Sacrament it is actually to visit Christ. God is everywhere— we have Him in our hearts—but in a special way He is in the chapel.

This religious sister claimed that the more your religious vocation developed, the more humble you became and the more dependent on God. She was a witness to the goodness and love of God and his sacrifice. The daily participation of the nuns in the Mass and their frequent visits to the Blessed Sacrament—the consecrated bread in the tabernacle—testify to these beliefs.

The Novice Mistress is a key functionary in the religious organization, for it is she more than any other who forms and tutors the young novices in the ways of religious life. She perpetuates the myth of foundation in her instruction. The Franciscan congregation have a particular strength in following St Francis. They hold dear the values of brotherly love and universal fellowship which other congregations had lost and searched to regain in the *aggiornamento* following the Second Vatican Council in 1965. The Novice Mistress explains, 'St Francis for his time was trying to be as Christ-like as possible. He was the most perfect man—love incarnate. When we say God is love we mean that everything he did was love, he talked to people with love and understanding.' The Franciscan message was, 'Go out and love your neighbour.' St Francis, like Jesus Christ, gathered a body of disciples about him who shared a communistic ideology and economy. In Weberian terms he was a 'charismatic' leader and his authority was legitimated by charismatic as well as by legal and traditional means. Just as the priest retains special powers through the pedigree of St Peter's relationship with Christ, so the authority figures in a Franciscan congregation carry a 'charismatic' quality in their leadership. The history of the Franciscan order is rich with mystical and magical confirmations of decisions taken and new organizations instituted.

In the chapel of the congregation I visited, there was a sacred symbol, a relic of St Francis. In the grounds of the convent there was a holy well. Franciscan spirituality which emphasizes spirit, ecstasy, inner will, not only enables the leader, the Mother General, to exercise a freedom of spirit and personality not given to organizations founded on more pragmatic and utilitarian grounds, but also provides a powerful aid in gaining the commitment of every member of the congregation to goals and values. The Franciscan congregation could be successful today because it had the means to avoid the more stereotyped devotional expressions of religious life common to other congregations, and it has been able to modify secondary goals according to the needs of the apostolate of the times. The Mass is still interpreted as a sacrificial feast because that interpretation is in complete accordance with the organization of daily life and ultimate goals. The Franciscan nun is part of a hierarchial organization with a charismatic leader at the top, a leader who embodies the mystical qualities of goodness and love. The nun devoted herself wholeheartedly to her organization, she mortifies her body with fasting and discipline. When she enters the convent chapel, in her pure white habit, sympol of her consecrated virginity, she enters a bright arena decorated with mystical scenes from the life of St Francis, his relic visible under a glass dome, a powerful protection against the evils and chaos of the world. The connection between her sacrifice, her founder/leader's sacrifice and God's sacrifice is complete. The god is indeed at the time sacrificer and victim, at one with the people for whom the sacrifice is offered.

The closeness between the participants in the Franciscan convent comprises one difference between it and the conservative teaching convent, but a more profound difference lies in the nature of personal sacrifice as understood in the two convents. Unlike the old teaching congregation, the Franciscans tried to develop and consecrate the talents of the nuns, rather than bury talent in total self-abnegation and mortification. The Franciscan emphasis is positive, rather than negative, egalitarian rather than differentiated by class and status. For them, the principal sacrificial symbol is the consecration of the victim.

V

One question that arises from these three interpretations of the Mass is why, in the teaching congregation, there occurred a shift from 'sacrifice' to 'communion'. One reason lies in the historical context. New ideas in the Catholic Church involve reinterpretations of the sacraments; traditional religious beliefs are widely questioned; authority—especially religious authority—no longer receives unquestioned recognition, and changes in the wider world give women more freedom, making more difficult to accept the total submission required in the old order. These changes in the wider world resulted in a dissatisfaction with the old rigid hierarchical structure of the congregation, which in turn resulted in a new understanding of its central rituals. The Franciscan congregation, however, which was relatively unaffected by changes in the wider world, provides a warning against too ready a satisfaction with the historical explanation. The context of the Mass in the lives of the nuns is also relevant.

The dramatic representation of the life of Christ in the words and symbols of the Mass has a sociological significance, relating to the execution of power and status in the various congregations. In the traditional teaching convent, the substitution of objects for real or imagined people constitutes a symbolic exchange confirming man's dependence on divine action to ward off evil and chaos, the anti-social forces of anomie. Such is the danger of this action that intermediaries are set up in strictly defined spatial zones. In the course of the sacrifice, there is destruction, real and symbolic. But the participants come away from the ceremony strengthened, both by the ingestion of sacred matter and by close comminication with the potent world of the gods. The priest is the key figure in this process: it is he who alone holds the power of consecration, the ability to unlock the channels of grace. It is he alone who drank the wine in the traditional scheme.

It is only when the relationships between Church authority and congregation changed, and the status of the priest was modified with respect to his audience, that the congregation could share fully in the communion. As the priest loses power and authority, the doctrine of transubstantiation falls into question, and the Mass reverts to a communion meal—a commemorative rite rather than a sacrifice. In the radicalism of the 1960s, when small groups took the significance of the Mass to be a celebration of their discrete membership, both convents Church lost members. People no longer needed the services of intermediaries. A rejection of self-abnegation in a rigidly hierarchical society led some to withdraw from the society, and others to restructure the society on egalitarian lines, expressed in a central rite of commensality.

The Franciscan congregation had a more flexible structure, which was hierarchical, but which respected the talents and traits of individuals. Their emphasis was on consecration of individuals rather than on the suppression of individuality. They had a corresponding interpretation of the Mass, which incorporated both the idea of death when this becomes necessary, and the commensal meal of a consecrated community.

Raymond Firth (1973: 425) commented that 'assertions about the bread and wine are assertions in defence of established positions or claims to such positions, on a pragmatic social level as well as on a conceptual level'. By treating religious ideas as social facts, I have come some way towards showing how, in the Mass, the articulation of ideas about this world and the next relate to the ordering of the social life of the convents.

NOTES

1. The identity of both congregations is disguised and the names of the nuns must have been changed, in an attempt to protect the privacy of all those who made the research possible. For a fuller account of the convents, see Campbell-Jones 1979. Strictly speaking, women who live in religious congregations under a simple vow are called 'religious sisters' or 'religious' (used as a noun). I have adopted the colloquialism 'nuns' for simplicity.

2. There is some correspondence between the three types of interpretation presented here and the 'root forms' of sacrifice which van Baaren (1964) puts forward. Van Baaren lists four such forms: a gift offering, either expecting reciprocity or offered in homage; parting with something of one's own for the benefit of another, emphasizing renunciation; repetition of a primordial event, often related to a ritual meal of renewal; and symbolic sanctification of the world, which often includes renunciation to a different end, and which is often linked to a ritual meal and a primordial event.

3. For a more detailed discussion of these points, see Campbell-Jones 1979: 102.

4. This fits in well with Robertson Smith's (cf. 1927: 312—3) 'communion theory' of sacrifice according to which sacrifice originally involved the killing of a sacred totemic animal, in some sense identified both with the deity and with the group which subsequently consumes it. The connection between symbolic killing and the sacrificial meal was examined by Leach (1972: 266) in his analysis of the Tongan *kava* ritual and myth: 'The eating of the meat of the sacrifice is deemed an

essential element in the rite; the congregation shares a collective guilt in participating in god murder and ritual cannibalism; this collective guilt is an 'atonement'; it makes the members of the congregation aware of themselves as a collectivity that has jointly sinned yet assimilated itself to God.' We should notice the intercessionary role of the nuns, also their adopted role of making reparation for the sins of mankind— in particular for the killing of the Son of God.

5. For a definition and explanation of 'plausibility' of religious beliefs, see Berger 1969: 26.
6. For a fuller exposition of this point, see Campbell-Jones 1979: 149—61.
7. The ambiguous nature of symbols is well exposed in Douglas 1970.

A COMMENSAL RELATIONSHIP WITH GOD: THE NATURE OF THE OFFERING IN ASSAMESE VAISHNAVISM

Audrey Hayley

Sacrifice as a field of study can be divided into two types. In the first (blood sacrifice), the object made sacred (*sacer*+*facio*) is a living creature and the central act of the rite is its immolation. In the second, the sacralized object is a vegetable offering rather than an animal victim and no ritual killing is involved. This distinction may itself be associated with our unfamiliarity with the public slaughter of animals, which leads us to place an excessive emphasis on the element of violence in blood sacrifice. At any rate, whether the gods are given offerings of vegetables or meat—and the former are increasingly being substituted for the latter nowadays—both types of sacrifice seem to use a similar grammar of procedures to effect common ends. In this paper I am concerned with one aspect of this field, namely the use of the alimentary system as a model of ritual interaction, which is discussed in respect of the offering among Vaishnavite devotional sects in Assam.

The path of *bhakti* or devotion which is based on the teachings of the Bhagavata Purana reached Assam as a religious movement towards the end of the fifteenth century. Today some eighty per cent of Assamese Hindus are estimated to follow this path, the remainder chiefly being *śakta* or worshippers of the consorts of Shiva. The distinguishing features of *bhakti* are the belief in a personal god conceived as a god of love and the choice of devotion to god as the easiest and most efficacious means of salvation. In Assam the adherents of *bhakti* are members of a Vaishnava sect founded by a non-Brahman called Shankaradeva who is regarded by his followers as an incarnation of god. The permanent organization of the sect takes two forms, the *satra* system under the authority of the *gurus* and the village Name House system controlled by the laity. A *satra* consists of a *guru* and the disciples initiated by him. It is supported by the annual tithes of the disciples and usually also by grants of revenue-free or half-revenue land made in the name of the *satra* idol. Some of the larger *satras* house celibate devotees who have

renounced the world, but the number of renouncers is few and the
movement is chiefly carried by the laity. Every man journeys to a
satra prior to marriage to take initiation, when the mysteries of the sect
are revealed to him in the form of esoteric *mantras*, and he continues
throughout life under the pastoral care of the *guru*. The disciples of a
satra, however, are usually widely scattered throughout the State so
that contact with the *guru* is necessarily remote and intermittent. The
village Name House, in contrast, provides the local community within
which its members ordinarily live their lives. In every village there is at
least one, and usually several, Name Houses whose members form a
'religious congregation' (Weber 1966: 60) consisting of a restricted
association of households who combine for the purpose of maintaining
a local centre of devotional worship. The Name House exercises not
only religious but also social and jural functions and, in the absence of
formal village and caste organisation, it constitutes the basic unit of
rural society in the greater part of the State. These two institutions
provide the framework of the sect.

The Assamese describe their religion as containing four things
(*cāri-vastu*)—Name, God, *Guru* and Devotee—which together form a
single and composite entity like the members of the Holy Trinity.
Following the convention adopted for the Trinity, I call these 'persons'.
At initiation the novice takes an oath surrendering himself to each of
the four persons in turn and all four are considered to be present both
in the performance of worship and in the offering. Devotional worship
is termed *sevā*, literally meaning obeisance or service, and is usually
carried out by a congregation singing hymns in the vernacular in contrast to Vedic or Brahmanical rites which are the monopoly of Brahman
priests versed in Sanskrit *mantras*. True *sevā* is disinterested in that it is
performed not as a means to an end but for the sake of the service
itself. If the motive for *sevā* is to obtain wordly gains or even spiritual
advancement, it ceases to be true *sevā*.[1] *Bhakti*, which originated as one
path to salvation (*mukti*) among others, later became valued as an end
in itself such that the devotee no longer desires salvation which he considers inferior to the state of ecstatic communion with Krishna.[2] The
Assamese, however, recognize that, because of human frailty, devotion
is not always—indeed not usually—undertaken for its own sake; and
for practical purposes they divide *sevā* into two kinds: *niskām*, literally
'without desire', which is motiveless, and *sakām*, literally 'with desire',
which is undertaken to gain a specific end. The great majority of performances fall into the latter category. The man at whose instigation
the *sakām* takes place and who pays for the offering is called the *sakāmī*
and it is to him that the benefits of the performance accrue.

Performances of this kind (*sakām*) are held for a great variety of purposes: to ensure success in the harvest, to prevent pots being broken in the firing, to attract a good catch of fish, to effect a safe delivery, to remove the baleful effects of birth or death at an inauspicious time, to appease the spirit of an ancestor, to pass an examination, to obtain a job, to cure sickness in the family, to mark the anniversary of a parent's death and at all *rites de passage*. The host invites to his house a number of devotees, ranging from a few neighbours to the entire membership of the Name House, who chant hymns, partake of the offering and utter blessings that the purpose of the rite be fulfilled. In some cases, especially protracted illness, it is usual to make a vow promising to give an offering or hold a feast for the devotees, provided that the sick man recovers. Occasionally the host does not reveal his purpose, and the blessing takes the form that what he desires in his mind may come to pass.

The act of worship, like the offering itself, is seen as a means of communion with god. The Vaishnavas conceive of heaven (*Vaikuṇṭha*) as an abode in the celestial regions above the world where Krishna sits surrounded by the company of his chosen devotees singing hymns to his praise. The purpose of worship is to recreate that situation here, namely to induce Krishna and his heavenly company to descend from their abode and take temporary residence in the bodies of the congregation. The Leader of the Prayer (*nām lagowā*) is installed as Krishna, the other devotees become invested with the heavenly host and the ingredients of the offering are transformed from the produce of this world into the articles of Krishna's granary. In a literal sense the aim is to create a heaven on earth. The place where the service is to be held is purified by smearing the ground with white earth, cow-dung and water and the congregation attend in a ritually pure state after bathing and putting on clean clothes. The Prayer Leader is required to fast beforehand. For worship, as for eating, a man wears three pieces of cloth, but no shirt. The Prayer Leader begins by establishing the *thāpanā*. *Thāpanā* literally means 'placing' and refers to the placing or invocation of Krishna into a sacred book, which is either the Bhagavat or one of the works written by the founding fathers of the sect which are in the main free translations from the Bhagavat. In Name Houses the scripture is a manuscript written on incense bark, in ordinary houses it is a book or paperback from the bazaar. The work is veiled from human sight by being wrapped in a cloth, and is placed on a raised bell-metal dish standing on the tip of a washed banana leaf to avoid contact with the ground. At the moment of placing the book on its stand the Prayer Leader utters a secret *mantra* taught him by his *guru* which has the effect of causing Krishna to take up residence in the book. The stand with its book now becomes a *thāpanā*, that is, an object inhabited by Krishna. It is said: 'In the *thāpanā* is god.' Thereafter no one should cross before it till the conclusion of the service. If it is necessary to do so, it is done stooping with the right hand pointing towards the ground. Near the base of the *thāpanā* the Prayer Leader places on banana leaves a dish of incense, a light of ghee or mustard oil, and a few annas with some uncut betel nuts on a pan leaf called the 'penalty offering' (*danda arccanā*), to which I return later. He now proceeds to the preparation of the offering.

The offering is called *prasād*, literally 'favour', or sometimes *māh prasād*, that is 'pulse offering', because of its vegetable content. The ingredients are whitish in colour as appropriate to an offering to Vishnu and, with the exception of ginger, are 'cooling'.[3] Ginger is said to be added because of its digestive properties. The articles used are washed and prepared beforehand by the Distributor. They consist of a fine variety of *lāhī* rice, two varieties of pulse (*but* and *magu*), bananas, pan leaves twisted into a funnel containing cut betel nut, segments of lime, coconut, ginger and salt and other fruits in season. The Distributor softens the rice and pulses by soaking them for a few hours in cold water.

The rationale of the offering is said to be based on the following lines of Shankaradeva, the founder of the sect, freely translated from the Bhagavat:

> If there is nothing in the world except Krishna
> I always worship Krishna with things full of Krishna;
> Seeing me Manu and all virtuous men
> Worship Hari with things in the form of Hari.

According to this view the phenomenal world is a manifestation of god and has no reality apart from him. He who makes the offering, the god to whom the offering is made, and the offering itself, exist only as his aspects. The realization of this identity is effected in the offering through *mantras*. The Prayer Leader squats on the ground facing east surrounded by the ingredients of the offering as washed and prepared by the Distributor, the rice in a basket or bowl on his right and the pulses on his left. He places on a banana leaf before (i.e. to the west of) the *thāpanā* a raised bell-metal dish and touches the base in salutation. In the bottom of the dish he puts a banana leaf. He then takes up four handfuls of rice followed by four handfuls of pulse—or two of rice and two of pulse alternately—and places them in the dish, uttering a *mantra* with each handful. The mound is then carefully patted for it is inauspicious for a grain to fall on the ground. The other ingredients are also used in fours (or multiples of four), that is, four bananas on the four sides, four funnels of pan and betel nut between the bananas, eight slices of coconut between the two, four segments of lime between the funnels and other fruits in season. As each ingredient is placed in the dish, he utters consecutively the *mantras*—*nām, guru, deva, bhakat*—one for each piece or handful. On the pinnacle he puts a pinch of salt, and on the salt ginger. The whole is covered with a banana leaf cut into an octagonal shape, which also has esoteric significance. There are minor differences of procedure according to the *guru* who imparted the instructions. By these *mantras* it is believed that each variety of food used in the offering is converted into the four persons whose names are uttered.

After completing his preparations, the Prayer Leader rises and walks backwards, dusting the ground before him with a banana leaf to remove the tread of his footsteps. He sits on a mat in the centre of the room facing the *thāpanā* to the east. The congregation has by now assembled and is already seated on the three sides, the senior and respected men occupying the upper places near the *thāpanā*. The Prayer Leader places the palms of his hands together and mentally utters the invocation (*arccanā*) which constrains Krishna, who is described as obedient to his devotee (*bhakatar baśya*), to leave *Vaikuntha* and become present in their midst. This consists of the secret name of god revealed to him by his *guru*. As a result of the invocation, the whole of *Vaikuntha* is translated to the place of worship. Krishna becomes present in the person of the Prayer Leader and the devotees who dwell in *Vaikuntha* descend to inhabit the devotees in the congregation. It was said: 'Krishna cannot leave devotee and devotee cannot leave Krishna. Krishna and devotee have one and the same body. Where there is devotee, Krishna always stays there.' From the invocation till the end of the service, no one must rise from his seat: to do so is equivalent to driving Krishna away and breaks the mystical union between god and devotee.

The response of Krishna to the invocation is assured by the reciprocal relationship between god and devotee. The love of the devotee for god is conceived on a number of models: as the tender love of a mother for her child when the infant Krishna is the object of worship; as the erotic love of a mistress for her lover in the Radha-Krishna cult of Bengal; as the submissive attachment of a servant to his master which is the prototype in Assam. Krishna, in turn, not only responds to the love of his devotees but positively desires it so that the relationship becomes reversible. As the devotee reaches out to Krishna, so Krishna is said to follow after his devotees and when one or two are gathered together in his name, he becomes present in their midst:

> I remain always in the company of my devotees and I do their bidding
> as if I were their slave (Shankaradeva: *Gopī-uddhave-saṁvāda*, 71, quoted
> by Neog 1963: 38).

Thus, although the devotee is submissive to Krishna, seeking shelter
at his lotus feet, Krishna is also described as inseparable from his
devotees and obedient to them.

The simplest service consists of hymns (taken from Madhavadeva's
Ghoṣā and Shankaradeva's *Kīrtan*) which are introduced by the Prayer
Leader and chanted by the congregation to the clapping of hands, a
reading from scripture (*Kīrtan*) by the Reader (*pāthak*), and some concluding religious instruction (*upodeś*) usually taken from *Daham*, a
rendering into Assamese of the tenth canto of the Bhagavat. The whole
service is called Name because it is an expression of the names or
attributes of god. If held for an individual purpose (*sakām*) the giver
of the Name, i.e. the *sakāmī*, bows down before the congregation at the
opening of the ceremony and declared its purpose (*sevā jānanī*). This
is repeated at the end, when a blessing is uttered that his wish be
fulfilled.

The formal offering (*arpaṇā*) is usually made by the Prayer Leader
after the hymns. The wording is not fixed but follows a traditional
pattern:

> At your feet, O Lord, has been placed one light on a stand, one dish of
> offering and one cut betel-nut. In this if there have been any errors or
> mistakes, wipe them all away and, accepting these articles as if from your
> own granary in *Vaikuntha*, may you be satisfied.

Thereupon Krishna is considered to become present (*stithi*) in the
offering. He purifies it (*śuci kara*), accepts it (*grahaṇ kara*) and eats it.
It thus becomes the residue of his food and is transubstantiated as
prasād, the 'favour' of god.

At the conclusion of the service the offering is distributed. The
Distributor first covers his mouth and nose with a cloth. He dismantles
the *thāpanā* by removing the sacred book: this symbolizes the departure
of Krishna who has finished eating. Members of the congregation are
now free to cross the room. He removes the cover from the offering and
returns each article to the basket from which it was taken, the four
bananas to the basket with bananas, the eight slices of coconut to the
basket with coconut, and so forth. The rice and pulses are placed in a
big brass bowl containing the remainder of the rice, pulses and salt,

and the whole is mixed thoroughly together. As a result of this contact the virtue of the sanctified food passes into all the food which becomes *prasād*. The Distributor then arranges portions of the *prasād* on sections of banana leaves and distributes them to the congregation, starting with the senior respected men. Portions should be offered and accepted with both hands and the Distributor, as a mark of respect, moves each leaf a little towards the person to whom it is assigned (*prasādar pāt diyā*). Consistent with the principle that all devotees are one and the same, all portions should be alike.[4] No one eats till all are served. *Prasād* must be entirely consumed and never thrown away. If not eaten immediately, it is taken home. The *prasād* of major festivals is sometimes kept for years, a little being taken after bath at the conclusion of a period of ritual pollution.

The significance of *prasād* has recently been analysed by Babb in terms of a hierarchical relationship between god and man evidenced by the fact that the worshippers eat 'the polluted refuse of the god with all its hierarchical implications' (Babb 1970: 297; 1975: 57). Babb argues that the prestation of food to the deity is a payment for past or future favours. At the same time, he says, a gift if unrequited debases the recipient so that reciprocity in some form must be incorporated in the ritual sequence in order to affirm the superior status of the god. This is effected by a counterprestation in the form of *prasād*. He points out that the food given to the god is superior food prepared under stringent conditions of purity, whereas the food received back by the worshippers consists of inferior and polluted leftovers. The eating of these leftovers as *prasād* restores the equlibrium that has been disturbed by the initial prestation so that, he says, 'the god has received payment *with* honor, and thereby the proper hierarchy has been maintained' (Babb 1975: 57). He concludes: 'An asymmetrical transaction in foods, then, lies at the heart of *puja* [in which he includes *sevā* or devotional worship, v. Babb 1975: 37—39], a transaction both expressive and supportive of hierarchical distance between the divine and the human' (Babb 1975: 57). The rest of his analysis is concerned with the sense of common identity among the participants that results from sharing the *prasād*, when caste divisions are temporarily suspended, 'reduced', as he puts it, 'to relative insignificance by the overwhelming inclusiveness of the hierarchical opposition between the mundane and the divine' (Babb 1957: 60).

This interpretation is misconceived in two respects. In the first place, it relies on a theory of gift-exchange derived from Mauss which is not applicable in the Hindu context. Hindu views on giving and receiving have recently been analysed by Van der Veen in relation to marriage patterns among Anavil Brahmans (Van der Veen 1972). Ideally a Hindu marriage is the 'gift of a virgin' made by the girl's father without any desire other than the making of the gift itself and received by the groom without any obligation to reciprocate. The effect of the marriage is to establish a hierarchical relationship between bride-giver and bride-receiver, such that the former is always subordinate to the latter and continues throughout life to honour the bride's affines by a continual stream of unrequited gifts. In reality of course men arrange the marriages of their daughters to obtain prestige and other worldly advantages, and much of Van der Veen's analysis is concerned with the ways in which the ideology of a pure gift and the denial of reciprocity is both realised and circumvented in practice. Gift-giving among the Asamese is an important part of the system of respect ($m\bar{a}n$) shown by inferiors to superiors. It is emphasized that a man's qualites pass with his gift, so that the acceptance of the gift, like the acceptance of food, is seen as a mark of favour. Brahmans who officiate at mortuary rites and accept gifts in the name of the dead are in an ambiguous position, becaue they take in and digest the dead man's sins. The gifts ($d\bar{a}n$) made to a priest for his services are always accompanied by a money payment ($daks\dot{i}n\bar{a}$) which is interpreted as a recompense to the priest for accepting the qualities of the donor in the gifts. Similarly, disciples are believed to transfer their sins to their *guru* by the payment of annual dues and a *guru* who does nothing to improve their spiritual condition is likened to a simul tree on which the disciples drop their sins as vultures drop their excrement. It is also emphasized that the act of giving is a completed act involving no counter-prestation. Should the recipient later make a gift to the donor, its connection with the original gift is denied on the grounds that, even if a man returns a gift tenfold he cannot rid himself of the qualities he accepted with the first gift. Babb's interpretation of *prasād* rests on the assumption that the giver is superior to the receiver. The Hindu gift is grounded on the opposite assumption that gifts pass from inferior to superior; and, in the case of marriage, it is the gift itself that establishes the superior ritual status of the son-in-law as recipient.

In the second place worship is not about rank, and the idiom of inter-caste food transactions is not an appropriate model to understand it. Between men, who are subject to defilement, food transactions are governed by considerations of ritual impurity. Food remains which have been in contact with the saliva are considered to contain the internal properties of the eater, and are accepted only from those of superior ritual status. In Assam junior kin will accept the food remains of senior kin without themselves becoming polluted, a son eating from the plate of his father or mother, a younger sibling from that of an older sibling and a wife from that of her husband. The cooking of food also opens it to ritual impurity, and the acceptance of cooked food implies that the donor is of the same or of superior status to the recipient. In the case of the offering the distributor softens the grain and pulses by soaking them beforehand for a few hours in cold water. According to Assamese notions, soaking, together with cutting open, husking and grinding, are classed as degrees of cooking in that they soften the food internally or open it to the outside so that the qualities of those who touch it pass into the food. The soaking of the grain is thus held to make it in some degree permeable to contagion. The *guru*, scrupulous in his food observances, will not accept *prasād* prepared by a distributor of a caste below Kalita, the highest *sudra* caste in Assam, and no man of clean caste will partake of the offering in the company of an Untouchable. Krishna, on the other hand, being a god, is not subject to ritual impurity and such considerations are not applicable to him. He is believed not only to accept and eat the offering of all true devotees, including Untouchables, but also to have expressed a desire to eat the food remains of his devotees:

> Nothing is superior to the food left by the devotee.
> I myself, O Arjuna, feel a craving to eat the remains of my devotee's
> food.

> (Quoted by Neog 1963: 11)

In general caste and other hierarchical distinctions are foreign to the spirit of *bhakti* and do not provide a basis for understanding the nature of the exchange symbolised in the offering by the giving and return of food. I approach this relationship through the 'penalty offering' (*daṇḍa arccanā*) mentioned above, consisting of a few annas with betel nut and pan placed on a banana leaf before the sacred scripture.

The performance of Name, as the service is called, aims to create a heaven on earth. This in the nature of things cannot be done perfectly, for the efforts of ordinary human beings necessarily fall far short of the divine model, and the 'penalty offering' is given in expiation of the gap between aspiration and performance. It is a token sum which underlines the 'token' value of all offerings to god. Those who take a leading part in the service—the host or *sakāmī* who gives the Name, the Prayer or Name Leader, the Scripture Reader and the Distributor of the offering—are required on the completion of their office to make an eight-point obeisance with the forehead on the ground while a prayer is uttered on their behalf in apology for their errors in performance: this is called the 'fault-breaking' (*aparādh bhānjan*). At the same time

Krishna is expected to accept the offering in spite of its imperfections and, by making it his own, to invest it with the qualities of *Vaikuṇṭha*:

> In the manner that the materials of *Vaikuṇṭha* should have been offered, in that manner it has not been possible to make the offering . . .

> Destroy all our faults and shortcomings; be pleased to consider the articles of the offering *as if from the granary of Vaikuṇṭha* and to accept it as your own.

> In this many faults have occurred . . . Make these faults faultless, wipe away the hundreds of shortcomings, be pleased to take this offering and say it is your own. *Being then satisfied with your own qualities*, may you show us kindness, O Lord.

> (Goswami: 29, 10, 29, freely translated; italics mine).

The assimilation of the human to the divine carries, on the human side, a sense of humility—'O Gobinda, I know not how to worship at your feet'—which has its counterpart in the concept of indulgence or divine grace—'Let god remove our faults and accept the offering as his own.' The transubstantiation effected in the offering by this creative exchange can be expressed in terms of a commensal model.

Through the offering the devotee enters into a commensal relationship with god. The offering is at once mental and material, consisting of an emotional attitude, termed devotion, which is held to be pleasing to god, and certain material substances which accompany and are the vehicle of this state of mind. Suppose we take D to denote the devotion, which term includes both the mental and material components of the offering, and K to denote Krishna. The distinguishing quality of Krishna is believed to be his love for his devotees—it is commonly said that Krishna is our greatest friend—and his accessibility to them. Then D passes into K where it is transformed or digested, to use an alimentary analogy, to become DK and, in this altered form, later re-ingested by the devotee. The effect of its sojourn in K is that K makes good the deficiencies in D by supplementing them with K qualities so that the DK re-introjected by the devotee is the product of the commensal mating within K of K and D. This is explicit in the words of the offering when Krishna is asked to accept the articles as if from his own granary in *Vaikuṇṭha* and thus to be satisfied with his own qualities. To change for the moment to a money analogy, the offering of the devotee represents token coinage which does not possess the intrinsic value for which it is current, the *prasād* of Krishna is this same coinage which has been given in at the bank in exchange for gold.

Communication with god is also effected by the utterance of his names. The concept of Name occupies a central place in Assamese

Vaishnavism which is often described as 'our religion of Name' (*āmār nām dharma*). The place of worship is called a Name House, the service largely takes the form of chanting the various names of Krishna and is itself referred to as Name, the esoteric knowledge revealed by the *guru* to the initiate chiefly consists of the secret names of god and their significance, and advanced devotees are provided with a rosary of one hundred and eight beads on which to tell the names of god as part of their daily ritual. In so far as the path of *bhakti* involves a participation of the individual in the divine through love, it presupposes the benevolence of a personal deity and his accessibility to those who approach him. The different names of god are considered to be expressions of his many aspects, epitomizing the qualities (*guna*) by which he can be known and reached, and represent the accessibility of god who out of love for his devotees opens himself to them. Since Krishna and his Name are held to be inseparable, whenever his Name is uttered Krishna is present automatically. By listening to Name the devotee is said to drink in Krishna through his ears, by uttering Name Krishna manifests in his mouth:[5] in this way he becomes filled with god. The names of god are described as a nectarine juice and can be regarded as a form of verbal food which is provided by Krishna for his devotees. 'Drink ye, drink ye, drink ye the ambrosial sweetness of Hari's name' (*Nām Ghosā* 704). In the case of the offering the relationship is commensal: the devotee eats god (in that his food remains are imbued with his qualities, *guna*). In the case of Name the relationship is verbal: the devotee speaks god (in that god's names represent his qualities, *guna*). Speech here substitutes for digestion. The offering consists of food provided by the devotees for god who by eating the food (D) invests it with K qualities so that it becomes DK. Name can similarly be regarded as verbal food provided by god for his devotees who drink the sounds (K) by uttering them whereupon they become KD. Whereas the offering represents the qualities of the devotees as received into Krishna, Name represents the qualities of god as received into the devotees. Here again the relationship is reciprocal. As the accessibility of god to man is the most highly valued of his qualities, the Name of god is said to be superior to god himself.[6] This raises the question of the role of the deity in *bhakti* and the extent to which man is considered dependent upon him.

The model of commensal relationship used above is taken from the work of W. R. Bion (v. Bion 1962: 35—36, 62, 90—94). Bion elaborated this model with reference to the mother/child situation where its usefulness to the child is evident. The efficacy of worship, however, cannot rest upon an analogous mechanism for, whereas the response of the

mother is real, the response of the deity is wholly imaginary. Herrenschmidt has proposed a shift of emphasis in the study of sacrifice from
the priest to the sacrifier and from the deity to the sacrificial process
arguing that the fruits of sacrifice are not held to derive from the god to
whom offering is made but from the act of offering itself (Herrenschmidt
1978: 7, 9). Our theistic bias towards religion has also been criticized
recently by Southwold who points out that we tend to characterize
and define religious phenomena in terms of a central concern with gods
or godlike beings whereas, in Buddhism at any rate (he argues), worship
of the gods, being usually directed to the attainment of worldly ends,
is associated with the profane and not the sacred and has no bearing
on the end of Buddhist striving (Southwold 1978).

This criticism also applies in the case of Hinduism where the
notion of 'divinity'—for want of a better term—is not the monopoly of
the large population of gods and goddesses who comprise the Hindu
pantheon and are the objects of worship. It is believed possible for man
to achieve a state of mind that enables him to participate in the divine
and thus to escape from the cycle of re-birth and attain salvation. The
same option is not open to gods who are incapable of mental development and are destined to be re-absorbed when the existing universe
completes its cycle at the end of the present Kali Yuga. The opposition
between gods and men is largely overcome by the belief that a man
participates in the god whom he worships: 'If I worship Krishna, I
become Krishna; if I worship a demon, I become a demon.' As a
result there is a tendency for the worshipper to substitute for god, a
development which appears to have taken place in Assamese Vaishnavism where supreme place is given, not to god, but to the religious
experience itself and to the devotee as the embodiment of that experience. The state of mind termed devotion requires a devotee (*bhakat*)
to experience the devotion, a god Krishna (*deva*) as the object of
devotion, a means of communication between god and devotee provided by god's names (*nām*), and a *guru* who, as the living god, acts as
the intermediary through whom the devotee relates to Krishna. These
four persons are held to be one and indivisible. Before the offering is
given to god, its ingredients are transformed by *mantras* into Name,
God, *Guru* and Devotee, or the four parts of devotion. It is devotion
itself that is offered to and accepted by god whose role as the object of
devotion is no more than a necessary part of the whole. The state of
devotion is most perfectly realized in the devotee. As a *guru* said:
'*Guru*, God, Name, all are found in the devotee. He is the embodiment
of them all.' In consequence the company of devotees is said to occupy
a position superior to god.

The following verse is often recited in the course of worship:

> 'Who worships Krishna alone without worshipping the devotees
> His offering Krishna does not accept as his own.
> Who in worshipping Krishna bows down to the devotees,
> His offering becomes *prasād*.'
>
> (Goswami:24)

Each of the four persons constituting devotion is an object of worship, and each receives special emphasis in one of the four sub-sects into which the *satras* are divided. In villages, where the congregations are ordinarily composed entirely of the laity, recourse is usually made to the devotees to deal with the everyday contingencies of life. Suppose a girl is suffering from a persistent illness. Her father may invite to his house a number of devotees noted for their piety to hold a *sakām* on her behalf. The Name Leader will utter a prayer to the devotees asking them to drive away disease, misfortune and death and to fulfil the desire of him who bows down before them. At the conclusion of the prayer the assembled company utter a great shout of 'O Hari, O Ram', and it is this endorsement by the devotees, termed the 'thunderclap of Hari' (Hari *dhbani*), which alone makes the prayer effective and realizes the purpose of the *sakām*. Worship of the devotees is held annually in the Name House when the congregation invite to a great gathering the entire membership of one or more Name Houses from the same or neighbouring villages. Each man has his feet washed on arrival before being carried to a place in the Name House. When he leaves his hosts bow down before him again and offer him gifts for he has come as a devotee 'in the form of god' (*eśwar rup*). It is said that even a child or a wicked man should be considered a devotee at that time and that all devotees are one (*eke*) and the same (*samān*). The prayers include some such words as these:

> As the company of devotees you are kings, you are the sacred Ganges, you are the bodily presence of the supreme god. We have not given you the welcome and farewell that you should have had . . . I should have carried you on my shoulders, but you came on foot. Here we have waited upon you and done you homage, bowing down before you in salutation and worship. All this has not been done as it should have been done. We have not even been able to offer you a piece of betel nut or a seat of grass. In this we have offended greatly. Remove our faults and, eating the betel nut from your own pocket, bless us your servants and grant us strength so that we can continue to worship you like this in the future (Goswami: 34—35, freely translated).

The form of address to the devotees does not differ significantly from the form of address to god, because it is considered that the true devotee by the continual practice of devotion has come to incorporate god. It is pointed out that the seating arrangements in many Name Houses, with the congregation in two facing rows, are such that when the congregation bow down in worship to god, they are at the same time bowing down in worship to one another. It is said: 'When the devotees are satisfied, god is satisfied.' In one of the sub-sects no *thāpanā* is established and the offering is set down before the assembled devotees themselves. Here the devotees substitute for the visible symbol of god, which is dispensed with altogether.

Prior to its realisation in experience, devotion is believed to exist in the devotee in the form of a state of mind waiting to be felt, like some valuable in a store to which he has not yet found access. The intervention of the *guru* is regarded as a necessary catalyst to the actualization of the experience. 'Without a *guru*,' Shankaradeva said, 'you cannot enter into my religion.' In the cooking of boiled rice, when the paraphernalia of cooking are ritually equated with cosmic phenomena, the *guru* is identified with the ladle which stirs the inert mass to action or with the fire which gives it momentum. Because the *guru* is seen as indispensable for the devotional experience, he is considered to exist in the experience itself as one of the four persons constituting devotion: as such the idea of the *guru* is invariably present in the enactment of worship and, if the *guru* himself is bodily absent, the Name Leader substitutes for him.

The legitimacy of the *guru* rests on a line of succession recorded in the family book of his *satra* which links him to the original founder of the sub-sect. The relationship between successive *gurus*, and ultimately between the founding *guru* and Krishna, is believed to be one of substantive identity. At initiation the novice is instructed to consider his *guru* as the embodiment (*murti*) of Krishna in whom he is seeking shelter. 'God and *guru* are one, different only in body.' Thereafter he is required to repeat daily after his morning bath the four secret names of god, termed 'worship of name' (*nām-sevā*) and the secret name of his *guru* as a form of Krishna, termed 'worship of the *guru*' (*guru-sevā*). In the sub-sect where devotion to the *guru* is particularly cultivated, the worship of images is forbidden on the grounds that the *guru* himself presents to his disciples the living image of god. The spiritual pre-eminence of the *guru* is expressed by the rule that, as he has no peer, no one can cook for him, but when he cooks all will eat. The food remains of the *guru*, like the food remains of god, are termed *prasād* and often sought after by those suffering from disease. A *guru* does not 'die' (*mare*), he 'passes on' (*cale*), for he is believed to attain salvation, and the place where his body is burnt becomes a shrine marked in some cases by a permanent structure credited with miraculous powers. The incorporation of the *guru* into the devotional experience is necessitated by his role as the mediator through whom the disciple draws near to god: as such he is more immediate to the disciple than the god he represents and is said to be superior to god.[7]

The importance attached in the sect to the idea of the *guru* is exemplified by the controversy over the *guru*ship. The founder of the sect, Shankaradeva, appointed his disciple, Madhavadeva, as his successor. The *satras* deriving from Shankaradeva's descendents by hereditary succession claim that the term *guru* should properly be used only of Shankaradeva. The *satras* deriving from Madhavadeva, on the other hand, name Madhavadeva as the real *guru* of the sect and consider Shankaradeva as an incarnation of god with whom, as the *guru* of their *guru*, their relationship is indirect and remote (Sarma 1966: 91, 98). In the main *satra* of this group the death aniversary of Shankaradeva is celebrated for seven days, while that of Madhavadeva is celebrated for ten days (Neog 1965: 345).

In this paper I have described the offering in Assamese Vaishnavism and attempted to analyse the four persons of the sacred reality held to be present in the offering in their relation to one another. The data seem to call for a reconsideration of the nature and role of the deity in *bhakti*. The devotional movement is usually described in theistic terms ('the theistic reaction', Bouquet 1966: 75; 'theism and devotion', Basham 1954: 328; 'monotheistic theism', Schweitzer 1951: 179). If devotional striving is to be seen as a form of theism, as we ordinarily understand the word, then the persons constituting devotion are valued in so far as they reproduce the character of god: god's Names indicate his qualities, the *Guru* is his representative on earth, the Devotee is the container in whom he becomes immanent. When, however, one or other of these persons is said to be greater than god, this approach fails.

Theism in the Hindu context is clearly different from theism as understood in the West. In spite of the emphasis in *bhakti* on a single anthropomorphic god as the only proper object of worship in this Kali age, the personal attributes of god are not considered to exhaust the divine principle, which exists within man as a microcosm of the universe. The conception of a personal god is indeed often considered less of a reality than a technique for realizing reality (cf. 'If god has no attributes, how am I to conceive of him?' Or, 'I worship this image of god. No, I do not worship this image. I place my *ātma* there and in the image I worship myself.') Whereas theism in Western thought is oriented to the personality of god in which man participates, devotion is oriented to the devotee as the embodiment of a divine principle more inclusive than the idea of god which it incorporates. The goal of devotional striving is not a god but a state of mind, termed devotion, conceived as the experience of love. One of the peculiarities of love is that it requires an object, even if the object is imagined, in other words it is only experienced as it is given away. Van Baal has suggested that the general characteristic common to sacrifice and offering is that both are gifts: he describes everyday offerings as 'vehicles of intentions' in which what is important, in the view of the offerer, is not 'who eats the offering', but the giving itself as a symbolic act (Van Baal 1975: 11, 170—171). Applied to devotional worship this interpretation suggests that the change effected in the offering is internal to the mind of the devotee. By virtue of their surrender to Krishna the ingredients of the offering, which are material possessions of the donor, undergo a qualitative change by acquiring the additional property of becoming a gift. Similarly the devotee, by the psychic act of bestowing the self on another, transforms his love from a latent capacity to a realized experience which incorporates as its object the image of god as a projection of the divine principle within him. The idea of Krishna as the object of worship may be placed in *Vaikuṇṭha*. More properly it is placed inside the devotee ('God is within your body: do not seek him elsewhere'). In so far as salvation in Hinduism is to be understood as the process of introducing a man to himself, the particular configuration of ideas in a religious experience can be viewed as an objective support for dispositions and tendencies which would otherwise continue to exist only as potentialities unavailable to the individual. From this viewpoint the 'truth' of the configuration rests on its evocative efficiency, which goes some way to explaining the importance attached to the role of the *guru*. It appears that in Hindu theism the emanations of a personalized god are encompassed by the belief in man's capacity to achieve his own divinity, an emphasis which supports the central position of the devotee not only as the container of god, but as the house of an in-dwelling state of mind in which god occupies only one of the four rooms.

ADDENDUM

The Sin-eaters: a note on the commensal model in relation to Hindu purification

The relation in Hinduism between the concepts of purity/impurity and sacred/profane has been insufficiently studied.[8] The nature of the purificatory process has also been little discussed in spite of widespread interest in the nature of impurity itself.

There seem to be two types of method for the removal of impurity: the action of the one is mechanistic and the other is digestive. Impurity itself may be external or internal to the object. External impurity can be conceived on the analogy of a film adhering to the surface and removable by washing away or burning off. This method is efficacious in respect of objects with a hard exterior like stone, iron or brass, and of the body polluted externally by contact with an impure substance or person. Porous objects such as clay vessels, cannot be ritually cleansed by this means because the impurity has penetrated inside and they are usually discarded after use. Similarly the eating of forbidden foods or a birth or death within the kin group sharing a common bodily substance results in internal impurity which cannot be reached by washing and for which burning is inappropriate. The committing of certain sins is also believed to produce a psycho-physical condition pervading the body. In these cases where mechanistic transfer is unavailable, recourse is made to the Brahman who in a literal sense is believed to digest the impurity without himself becoming impure. The capacity to assimilate pollution does not derive from the superior purity associated with the caste status of the Brahman which, on the contrary, renders him vulnerable to sources of contagion disregarded by less pure castes. Purity, being an empty or vacuous state, has no positive content with which to resist the penetration of impurity and can be maintained only by vigilance, withdrawal and avoidance.

I suggest that the role of the Brahman as the absorber of pollution inheres in the sacred nature of his Brahmanhood, which enables him, without impairment, to take into himself the sins and impurities of his clients through the gifts they make as payment for his services. In the ritual removal of impurity (*prāyaścitta*) the priest invokes into the purificatory water (*śānti pānī*) five gods, the seven sacred rivers and the five products of the sacred cow. This is sprinkled on the body to cleanse it outside and drunk to cleanse it inside. The action of the sacred may be considered as that of digesting the impurity (on the model of the alimentary system) or of containing the impurity (on the model of the container and the contained).

The role of the Mahabrahmans in absorbing the spiritual impurities of the dead is discussed by Parry (Parry, forthcoming). These funerary specialists are made consubstantial with the deceased by accepting the gifts made in his name so that they take his sins upon themselves. In theory, he says, they destroy these sins by digesting them and thus maintain their own status unimpaired. He continues: 'But as the priests themselves see it, the actuality is quite different. Since they cannot really 'digest' the sins they accept, so far from being paragons of purity, they regard themselves as cess-pits for the wickedness of the cosmos. The consequence of this accumulation of sins is that the priest faces the prospect of a lingering death from the rotting effects of leprosy, or even—in the case of certain particularly 'indigestible' kinds of offering—an immediate demise' (Parry, forthcoming). Much of Parry's analysis is concerned with the ambiguous position of the Mahabrahman, whose livelihood depends on the acceptance of gifts, while the spiritual properties required to deal with the gifts are considered to be eroded if the gifts are accepted not disinterestedly but for material gain. Although the office of the priest in the removal of sin is here compounded by human frailty and greed, it appears that one aspect of the complex relation of the sacred to the pure in Hinduism is conceptualized as the capacity of the sacred to digest impurity on an explicitly alimentary model.

Similar ideas are to be found in the sin-offerings and guilt-offerings of the Old Testament which were eaten by the priest (Snaith 1967: 16—17, 57, 117), and in the old English custom of hiring a sin-eater at funerals who was given sixpence together with a loaf of bread and a bowl of beer to consume over the corpse, 'in consideration whereof he tooke upon himself (ipso facto) all the Sinnes of the Defunct' (Aubrey 1881: 35).

ACKNOWLEDGEMENTS

I am grateful to Richard Burghart and Adrian Mayer for their helpful comments on an earlier draft of this paper and to Jonathan Parry for kindly making available to me his forthcoming paper on the Mahabrahmans of Benares. To my mentor, Dr. Piatigorsky, I owe a special debt for his radical criticisms.

NOTES

1. Adrian Mayer has elaborated the implications of this distinction in relation to public service in his paper, 'Public service and individual merit in a town of central India' (Mayer, in press).
2. Cf. the opening lines of Madhavadeva's *Nām ghoṣā*: 'I salute the devotee who has no desire for salvation.'
3. The Assamese categorize food as 'heating' and 'cooling'. Heating foods are held to raise the temperature of the blood and excite the passions and are offered to female goddesses embodying the *śakti* of Shiva. Cooling foods, which lower the temperature of the blood and calm the mind, are offered to Vishnu.

4. Parry draws attention to *bhakti* as one of the areas stressing egalitarian values within the hierarchical world of caste (Parry 1974: 116—118). The absence of distinction between devotees during the performance of worship appears to support this view, as does the organization of the Name House, where each household contributes equally, both in money and in labour, to the cost of construction and to the celebration of festivals. I am not, however, convinced that the concept of equality is applicable here. The fact that all devotees are considered be to in some respects one and the same seems to exclude the possibility of their equality, for in so far as persons are identical they cannot be thought of as equal. The Western concepts of hierarchy and equality are substituted in the Hindu context by the distinction between those who share the same moral substance and those of different moral substance. It can be questioned whether imported categories such as hierarchy, equality, individualism or, as I discuss later, theism, are appropriate to an understanding of the conceptual order of Hinduism.

5. Cf. 'The mouth that utters Ram is the repository of Ram' (*Nām ghoṣā* 451).

6. Cf. 'Thy name is superior to thee' (*Nām ghoṣā* 637).

7. *Guru*-worship is also highly developed in the *bhakti* sect of Vallabhacharya where the superiority of the *guru* to god is explained on the principle that 'the bestower of the gift is greater than the gift' (Peter Bennett: personal communication).

8. Some of the obscurities in this area have been raised by Veena Das and Jit Singh Uberoi in a brief contribution to the symposium on *Homo hierarchicus* published in *Contributions to Indian sociology*, new series, V, 1971.

POSTSCRIPT: A PLACE FOR SACRIFICE IN MODERN CHRISTIANITY?

S. Barrington-Ward and M. F. C. Bourdillon

The conference on sacrifice from which this collection of essays emerged was intended to explore common ground between anthropologists on the one hand, and biblical scholars and churchmen on the other. Among the reasons for choosing 'sacrifice' as a topic was an apparent presumption of recent theology that 'modern man' has no need of such a symbol (*Royal Anthropological Institute News* **28**: October 1978). We now ask, is there any connection between, for example, Dogon sacrificial rites which aim to release supernatural force through the letting of blood (cf. Dieterlen 1976), and the ritual ways in which Christians seek to express the centrality of the sacrifice of Christ? Does either set of rites and stories have any place in a 'modern' society which claims to replace ritual and belief with rational action and science?

To deal with the former question first, in each case 'sacrifice' dramatizes themes which are central to the performers' understanding of their life in the world. The rites connect with fundamental myths about the creation of the world, order and disorder within it, and the constant need to restore order. In each case, sacrificial rites express ideal social relations: the ideal social structure of Dogon society in the one case; an ultimate and universal community of love in the other. In coming together for a sacrificial rite, people express an acceptance of the principal cosmological symbols, and of the moral ideals, which the prescribed ritual contains. There are at least some functional parallels between traditional Dogon sacrifice and contemporary Christian language and practice.

Yet clearly there are also great differences. Although Christians use a number of the symbolic meanings appropriate to sacrificial killing —often transmitted through Old Testament stories—Christian rites do not incorporate physical death: indeed, the focus is on the victim's self-offering culminating in his acceptance of death, rather than on the act of killing. In discussion relating to sacrifice in the modern world,

Francis Groot spoke from his missionary experience among the Luo of Kenya on the difficulty of conveying to traditional Luo the Christian idea of sacrifice. He pointed out that Christian sacrificial symbolism is as foreign to them as it is to people in modern western societies.

This could mean, however, no more than that every tradition of sacrifice is culturally specific, to be understood only in the context of a given system of symbols. The Luo are likely to have difficulty in understanding Dogon sacrifice. We might draw attention to the incomprehension of traditional Lugbara when they were told that the Nuer sometimes substitute a wild cucumber for the sacrificial ox: the Lugbara asserted that their spirits were not so stupid as to be cheated in that way (Middleton 1960: 88). Christians are certainly not unique in using sacrificial symbolism without ritual killing: the Tonga of the South Pacific, for example, also have a ritual meal which is explained in terms of a mythical sacrifice (Bott 1972; Leach 1972).

Is this then to imply that Christian sacrifice is simply a symbolic myth with its attendant rituals, to be analysed as an equivalent to the myths and rituals of any other religious system? In one sense, yes: such a view is presupposed in the kind of study presented in this volume. But a presupposition of the meeting between anthropologists and theologians is that Christian sacrifice has a special claim to interest on account of the historical place of Christianity in the evolution of the western civilization.

Clearly to Christians, Christian sacrifice is unique in another sense. To the people who use sacrificial symbolism, their own sacrifices uniquely express ways in which they understand their world. What follows is to some extent such a view from within a symbolic system. To Christians, it offers a contemporary way of understanding sacrifice. To others it is a piece of ethnography, indicating how Christian religious specialists may view their myth and ritual, with some important implications for the understanding of sacrifice in plural societies.

To Christians, the sacrifice of Christ is a key to their understanding of life, and thence of all other sacrifices. For them, the life and death of Christ is the central, final and universal sacrifice, at which other attempts at sacrifice may hint directly or indirectly. Christ is seen as 'a lamb slain from the foundation of the world' (Revelation 13:8). For Christians, this sacrifice integrates many of the meanings that have been attributed to sacrifice: gifts or offering to God; restoration of order against the forces of death and evil, mediated by the Divine King; the substitution of a life for other lives; the precondition of the ultimate banquet of 'the kingdom'; the complex interrelation of power and life with suffering and death. The sacrifice of Christ is seen by Christians as the fusion and fulfilment of Old Testament sacrifices, and it stands in an analogous relationship to the sacrifices of other cultural traditions.

This Christian understanding of sacrifice does not in any way carry with it the corollary that Christians should, as some missionaries have done, disregard the significance which those of other world views give to their own sacrificial myths and rites. Rather it posits in the sacrifice of Christ an inclusive symbol, transcending other more restricted forms of sacrifice. Such an understanding necessarily risks the charge which sometimes surfaced within the conference itself of ethnocentricity.

Christians must acknowledge the truth of this charge as a critique of many recent western Christian attitudes and actions. But there is a feature of this implicit comprehensiveness which clearly differentiates Christian sacrifice from, say, Dogon sacrifice. The former has been compelled, both by the comprehensiveness of its claim and by its wide dispersion in human history, to seek continually more universal forms of expression. From the very beginnings of the Church, between East and West, Christians have repeatedly tried to re-interpret their world of meaning in terms of symbols which are not specifically Christian (notice Sykes's reference to Shakespeare's *Measure for Measure*). As a result, Christian symbols are used by a wide variety of peoples. Whether as a cause or result of this widespread use, Christian symbols necessarily focus on problems which are widely experienced.

What now about the relevance of these symbols to 'modern man'? Some argue that Christianity essentially involves a 'spiritualization' of sacrifice, a movement away from a primitive emphasis on the correct performance of sacred rituals (cf. Daly 1978; Segundo 1964). If this were the case, perhaps the logical conclusion of the movement would be to drop ritual altogether. Here we touch on two further features of Christian sacrifice, which may have implications in other areas of symbolic action.

The first is inherent in the form of the central theme and story, the sacrifice of Christ. Christian faith emerged at a moment in the history of the Mediterranean basin, when the many jostling religions and cults of the Hellenistic and Roman world were undergoing a widespread process of spiritualization (see McKelvey 1969). Within Judaism we can see that process at work in the subtle allegorizing by which Philo reinterpreted Temple rituals in terms of individual moral and emotional states. We can also see it in a widespread emphasis among Rabbis— and even among such extreme traditionalists as Qumran community (Gartner 1965)—on keeping the law as itself a sacrifice, a tendency which greatly alleviated the pain of the destruction of the Temple in AD 70. But the peculiar Judaeo-Christian mode of development did not spiritualize away the essentially localized, concrete focal points of faith and worship. The specific symbols of the Jewish sacrificial cult were not totally lost in general abstractions. Something of their particularity and definite material quality was retained through the emphasis on the historical life and death of a particular person. In this new form, the sacrificial symbols carried more emphasis on their spiritual and ethical implications, and could be applied beyond the limits of the strictly Jewish cult.

The second feature, a corollary of the first, finds expression in the complexity of the relationship between the main Christian rites, sacraments as they came to be called, and the original historical sequence— the primal rite of the self-offering of Jesus Christ as priest and victim. Baptism and Eucharist alike were seen as essentially a participation in that prior self-offering. Thus to treat the Eucharist—or the Mass, as it became—simply as a Christian sacrifice has its difficulties. A certain literalism and rigidity in late medieval eucharistic theology (doubtless a sympton of a social situation still in need of proper analysis), inherited as much by Protestants as by Tridentine Catholics, led to a bitter conflict in the Reformation precisely over this point. Was the Mass a sacrifice at all, and if so in what sense? Protestants maintained that since the sacrifice of Christ was universal and final, there was little room in the Mass for more than a bare commemoration of Christ's death; Catholics tended to define the Mass as a repetition (for a good brief account, see Chapter 4, Mascall 1953). In the present century (in a changed social context), Catholic and Protestant theologians have drawn closer to a consensus. (For a Protestant development of the theme, see Moule 1956.) The sacrifice of Christ is now held to be constituted not so much in his death alone, as in his whole self-giving set in the hard conditions of our existence, in a life of love even at the cost of death. The sacrament of the Mass becomes, like other Christian sacraments, a realisation and application of Christ's self-giving. The symbolic action is an appropriation of the whole original event of Christ's birth, life, death, resurrection and ascension, by which the worshippers participate in that total offering.

Both these historical sequences indicate that for Christians sacrifice is still very much a vital and relevant reality, which if it is to be understood metaphorically, endows the notion of metaphor with unaccustomed intensity and unitive power, analogous to the power released by the religious rites with which anthropologists are familiar. The sacrifice of Christ retains something of the literal force of more localized, culturally confined and physically destructive symbolic acts so common among peoples throughout the world. For Christians it has universal application, yet remains a concrete symbol. This may be a clue to the difficulties encountered both by the Luo and by modern western man in coming to terms with it.

At the conference, Professor J. E. Burkhart argued that the spritualization of sacrifice arises from religion in modern society having become more and more a private, individual concern, and no longer creating true social links between adherents. He argued that this is connected to much of the rootlessness that is felt in modern society, and he made a strong plea for a renewed emphasis on Christian sacrifice as a symbolic community meal. This is one tenable approach to the question. But it does not necessarily apply to those who value the independence of life and thought that the modern world offers, and who find that their community needs are adequately filled without the ritual meal. Even those who accept the social need for commensality may ask whether the Christian form of ritual meal is adequate for the purpose. In any case, the need for commensality does not explain the need for the symbol of sacrifice.

Perhaps here we can refer back to the anthropological data on sacrifice, and notice that very often sacrifice is performed in some kind of crisis. The Dogon sacrifices aim to restore a meaningful order which is threatened by some calamity. Many sacrifices are performed to avert the threat of death, particularly in time of illness. We might regard sacrifice in such circumstances as an attempt to hold on to order and meaning when things are going wrong. It is precisely in such threatenning circumstances that many in the modern world resort to religious ritual.

It is the more joyful type of sacrifice which is under greater threat. In a small-scale traditional society, in which there is a commonly accepted world of meaning, sacrifice is often performed on occasions of great solemnity or celebration in an assertion of this established world of meaning. In a modern plural society, however, there is no commonly accepted world of meaning, and only material goods are sufficiently widely accepted to be useful for celebration. In such a society, sacrifice is a form of celebration for small, relatively exclusive groups only.

If the case for sacrifice can be sustained only on the basis of a particular view of the world—whether the view of, say, a traditional African community, or that of Christians of a particular time and place —any attempt to maintain its worth in the modern world seems doomed to failure. No myth and no symbolic action can have unquestioned validity in a relativist setting. It would seem that it is only if some vague yet persistent sense of transcendence, some 'rumour of angels' (as Peter Berger, 1970, expresses it), infiltrated the ruins of failing patterns of belief and practice, would modern man be able to respond to Christian symbols—uncertainly, and even wistfully. The Christian world of meaning responds in a way that has parallels in the divine sacrifices of other religious traditions (see Hubert and Mauss 1964: 77—94). It posits as the supreme sacrifice a divine self-offering, by dint of which divinity itself was exposed to the dereliction of our own uncertain questionings and conflicts, to open up the possibility of a *sacrificium*, a 'making holy' of the offerings of men. Even the possibility of such vulnerable divinity evokes a response which is not out of place in the modern pluralist world.

All people have some fundamental values about human life and about our responsibilities to others, based perhaps on an instinctive need for the security of society. Yet the lives of most peoples, in any society, are largely filled with regular and inescapable activities, necessary to keep alive and in as much comfort as possible—which often implies competition with others rather than responsibility towards them. Occasions for putting into practice fundamental social values are not part of the habitual activity of daily life. It could be argued that in the fluidity of a plural society, values are especially insecure and dependent on chance social circumstances. Yet there have been episodes in human history which warn of the danger of letting fundamental social values or instincts die: the tacit support of a nation for the crimes perpetrated by the Nazi movement is one extreme example. History has repeatedly shown that times of extreme privation, particularly with the threat of starvation, have led to a breakdown of any sense of social obligation. In such extreme cases, a sacrificial response seems to be required to restore a threatened order. It could be argued that when society is threatened in lesser ways, an analogous sacrificial response is appropriate.

How can a person be orientated and prepared for such a response? How are we to keep our fundamental values and instincts alive in our pool of habitual responses? First perhaps, through the symbolic enactment in some form or another of what in Christian symbols is expressed as that divine renunciation of security. It is suggested in much serious literature, painting, theatre and cinema. There has always been an association between religion and art. But even in the miraculous transformation of sensibility which art can affect, there is inevitably a danger of too great a passivity, of giving what is not much more than a notional assent to the message conveyed. Another means, widely established throughout human history, of both communicating such a fundamental demand and releasing the energy to react adequately, is through the deliberate and reflective performance of religious rites. The regular presentation of the call to sacrifice, through the dramatic recalling of a divine self-giving, increases the likelihood of being able to respond at the crucial moment.

There is a suggestion that one of the functions of religious rites is to provide for the participants a kind of conditioning or training. An analogy is the importance given to ceremonial in much military training, which is geared to produce controlled reactions in times of great crisis, and which traditionally includes many difficult and often stressful exercises which have no immediate usefulness. Similarly, in times of persecution, Christians who anticipated torture and martyrdom have sometimes prepared themselves by taking on a rigorous and severe discipline of ritual, accepted in the symbolic idiom of sacrifice.[1] This is an extreme case, but it does give a hint as to the response that sacrificial ritual can release in people in a time of crisis.

When a Nuer man, on seeing his byre struck by lightning and catch fire, first speared an ox in sacrifice to God before rescuing his family and cattle (Evans-Pritchard 1956: 205), he was in effect saying that there was something more important to him than all he stood to lose. When a Christian puts aside half an hour of a busy day for the sacrifice of the Mass, he is asserting, to himself as well as to others, that the story of the life, death and resurrection of Christ points to something more profound in his own life than all the flux of opinions, aspirations and regrets, the enjoyment and the tedium, that make up so much of it.

NOTES

1. A study of the use of ritual to such ends is given in Byman 1978. We do not, however, accept that Byman has established the pathological nature of the rituals he describes, nor the influence of a suppressed 'suicide urge' among the Tudor Martyrs.

NOTES ON CONTRIBUTORS

SIMON BARRINGTON-WARD
General Secretary of the Church Missionary Society, he has worked in Nigeria for three years on the staff of the Religious Studies Department of the University of Ibadan. On his return to Britain he became first Fellow and Dean of Chapel at Magdalene College, Cambridge, and later Principal of the CMS college, Crowther Hall at Selly Oak.

JOHN BEATTIE
Fellow of Linacre College, Oxford. Formerly Senior Lecturer in Social Anthropology at Oxford University and more recently Professor of African Studies at the University of Leiden. Author of *Other Cultures*, *The Nyoro State*, and other writings in social anthropology and in the ethnography of the Banyoro of western Uganda.

MICHAEL BOURDILLON
Jesuit priest and Senior Lecturer in Sociology, University of Zimbabwe. Author of *Shona Peoples*, and other writings in the social anthropology of religion and in the ethnography of the Shona peoples of Zimbabwe.

SUZANNE CAMPBELL-JONES
At present with BBC Open University Productions. She has a Ph.D. in sociology and is the author of *In Habit: A Study of Working Nuns*.

MEYER FORTES
Was William Wyse Professor of Social Anthropology at the University of Cambridge from 1950 to 1973, and a former President and Huxley Memorial Medallist of the Royal Anthropological Institute. He is a Fellow of the British Academy.

AUDREY HAYLEY (*Audrey Cantlie*)
Lecturer in Sociology with reference to South Asia at the School of Oriental and African Studies, London and has a special interest in the relationship between anthropology and psychoanalysis.

C. T. R. HAYWARD

Previously Lecturer in Jewish Studies in the Department of Religious Studies at Lancaster University; and has been Lecturer in Old Testament in the University of Durham since 1979.

JOHN W. ROGERSON

Professor of Biblical Studies, University of Sheffield. Previously taught in the Department of Theology, University of Durham. His books include *Myth in Old Testament Interpretation* and *Anthropology and the Old Testament*.

STEPHEN SYKES

Has been Van Mildert Canon Professor of Divinity, Durham University, since 1974 and is the author of *Friedrich Schleiermacher* and *Christian Theology Today*.

BIBLIOGRAPHIC REFERENCES

Albeck, H. 1954. *Shisha Sidre Mishnah, Seder Mo'ed.* Jerusalem.

Arinze, F. A. 1970. *Sacrifices in Ibo Religion.* Ibadan: Ibadan University Press.

Aubrey, J. 1881. *Remaines of Gentilisme and Judaisme* (ed.) James Britten. London.

Babb, L. A. 1970. The food of the gods in Chhattisgarh. *S.W. Journal of Anthropology* **26**, 387—304.

———— 1975. *The Divine Hierarchy.* New York: Columbia University Press.

Barrett, C. K. 1971. *A Commentary on the Epistle to the Romans.* London: A. and C. Black.

———— 1972. Mark 10.45: A ransom for many. In *New Testament Essays.* London: SPCK.

Bartchy, S. S. 1979. Table Fellowship with Jesus and the 'Lord's Meal' at Corinth. In *Increase in Learning: Essays in Honor of James G. van Buren* (ed.) R. J. Owens *et al.* Kansas: Manhattan College Press.

Basham, A. L. 1954. *The Wonder that was India.* London: Sidgwick and Jackson.

Battenhouse, R. 1946. *Measure for Measure* and the Christian doctrine of the Atonement. *Publications of the Modern Language Association of America* **61**, 1029—59.

Beattie, J. H. M. 1960. On the Nyoro concept of *Mahano. African Studies* 19 (3), 145—50.

———— 1964. The ghost cult in Bunyoro. *Ethnology* **3** (2), 127–51.

———— 1969. Spirit mediumship in Bunyoro. In *Spirit Mediumship and Society in Africa* (ed.) J. Beattie and J. Middleton. London: Routledge and Kegan Paul.

Berger, P. 1969. *The Social Reality of Religion.* London: Faber and Faber.

———— 1970. *A Rumour of Angels: Modern Society and the Rediscovery of the Supernatural.* New York: Doubleday.

Berreman, G. D. 1969. Bringing it all back home: Malaise in Anthropology. In *Reinventing Anthropology* (ed.) D. Hymes. New York: Pantheon Books.

Bion, W. R. 1962. *Learning from Experience.* London: Heinemann.

Bloch, M. 1977. The past and the present in the present. *Man* (new series), **12**, 278—92.

Blunt, A. W. F. n.d. *Helps to the Study of the Bible* (2nd ed.). Oxford: Oxford University Press.

Bott, E. 1972. Psychoanalysis and ceremony. In *The Interpretation of Ritual* (ed.) J. S. La Fontaine. London: Tavistock.

Bouquet, A. C. 1966. *Hinduism.* London: Hutchinson University Library.

Bourdillon, M. F. C. 1978. Knowing the world or hiding it: a response to Maurice Bloch. *Man* (new series), **13**, 591—99.

―――― 1979. The cults of Dzivaguru and Karuva amongst the North Eastern Shona peoples. In *Guardians of the Land* (ed.) M. Schoffeleers. Gwelo: Mambo Press.

Bradbury, R. E. 1973. *Benin Studies*. London: Oxford University Press.

Brown, C. 1978. Sacrifice. In *The New International Dictionary of New Testament Theology*. Exeter: Paternoster Press.

Brown, N. O. 1966. *Love's Body*. New York, Vintage Books.

Bulmer, R. 1973. Why the cassowary is not a bird. In *Rules and Meanings* (ed.) M. Douglas. Harmondsworth: Penguin Education.

Buxton, J. 1973. *Religion and Healing in Mandari*. Oxford: Clarendon Press.

Byman, S. 1978. Ritualistic acts and compulsive Behaviour: The pattern of Tudor Martyrdom. *American Historical Review* **83** (3), 625—43.

Calvin, J. 1853. *Commentaries on the Last Four Books of Moses*, 2. Edinburgh.

Campbell-Jones, S. 1979. *In Habit*. London: Faber and Faber.

Cartry, M. 1976. Le statut de l'animal chez les Gourmantché (Haute-Volta), première partie. In de Heusch (ed.) 1976, *q.v.*

Colleyne, J.-P. 1976. Le sacrifice salon Hubert et Mauss. In de Heusch (ed.) 1978, *q.v.*

Cornelius à Lapide. 1523. *Commentaria in Pentateuchum Mosis*. Antwerp.

Couratin, A. H. 1969. Liturgy. In *The Pelican Guide to Modern Theology*. Harmondsworth: Pelican Books.

Daly, R. J. 1977. The soteriological significance of the sacrifice of Isaac. *Catholic Biblical Quarterly* **34** (1), 45—75.

―――― 1978. *The Origins of the Christian Doctrine of Sacrifice*. London: Darton, Longman and Todd.

Danby, H. 1933. *The Mishnah*. Oxford: Clarendon Press.

Davies, Douglas 1977. An interpretation of sacrifice in Leviticus. *Zeitschrift für die alttestamentliche Wissenschaft* 89, 387—99.

Davies, P. R. 1979. Passover and the dating of the aqedah. *Journal of Jewish Studies* **30**, 59—67.

―――― and B. D. Chilton 1978. The Aqedah: a revised tradition history. *Catholic Biblical Quarterly* **40**, 514—46.

Denzinger, H. 1967. *Enchiridion Symbolorum, Definitionum et Declarationum de rebus et Morum* (ed.) A. Schönmetzer. Rome: Herder.

Dieterlen, G. 1976. Introduction à de nouvelles recherches sur le sacrifice chez les Dogon. In de Heusch (ed.) 1976, *q.v.*

Douglas, M. 1966. *Purity and Danger*. London: Routledge and Kegan Paul.

―――― 1970. *Natural Symbols*. London: Cresset Press.

―――― 1975. *Implicit Meanings*. London: Routledge and Kegan Paul.

Driver, G. R. 1963. Leprosy. In *Hastings Dictionary of the Bible* (ed.) F. C. Grant and H. H. Rowley. Edinburgh: T. and T. Clark.

Durkheim, E. 1912. *Les formes élémentaires de la vie religiux : le système totemique en Australie.* Paris: Alcan. (Trans. 1915. *Elementary Forms of Religious Life.* London: George Allen and Unwin.)

Dussaud, R. 1921. *Les origines Cananéennes du sacrifice Israélite.* Paris: Ernest Leroux.

Edel, M. and Edel, A. 1968. *Anthropology and Ethics* (rev. ed.). Cleveland: Press of Case Western Reserve University.

Evans, C. F. 1970. *Resurrection and the New Testament.* London: S.C.M. Press.

Evans-Pritchard, E. E. 1956. *Nuer Réligion.* Oxford: Clarendon Press.

Firth, Raymond 1961. *Elements of Social Organization.* London: Watts and Co.

—— 1963. Offering and sacrifice: problems of organization. *Journal of the Royal Anthropological Institute* **93** (1), 12—24.

—— 1964. *Essays on Social Organisation and Values.* London: Athlone Press.

—— 1973. *Symbols Public and Private.* London: Allen and Unwin.

Fortes, M. 1959. *Oedipus and Job in West African Religion.* Cambridge: Cambridge University Press.

—— 1975. Tallensi Prayer. In *Studies in Social Anthropology: Essays in memory of E. E. Evans-Pritchard by his former Oxford Colleagues* (ed.) J. Beattie and G. Lienhardt. Oxford: Clarendon Press.

Frazer, J. B. 1890. *The Golden Bough.* London.

—— 1911. *The Magic Art and the Evolution of Kings,* 1 (*The Golden Bough,* 3rd ed.). London: Macmillan.

—— 1913. *The Scapegoat.* (*The Golden Bough,* 3rd ed.) London: Macmillan.

Frye, R. M. 1963. *Shakespeare and Christian Doctrine.* Princeton: Princeton University Press.

Gartner, B. 1965. *The Temple and the Community in Qumran.* Cambridge: Cambridge University Press.

Geiger, A. 1872. Erbsünde und Versönhungstod: Geren Versuch in das Judenthum einsurdringen. *Jüdische Zeitschrift für Wissenschaft und Leben* **10**, 166—71.

Gerhardsson, B. 1974. Sacrificial service and Atonement in the Gospel of Matthew. In *Reconciliation and Hope* (ed.) R. J. Banks. Grand Rapids (Mich.): Eerdmans.

Girard, R. 1977. *Violence and the Sacred.* (Trans.) London and Baltimore: Johns Hopkins University Press.

Goldenweiser, A. A. 1932. *History, Psychology and Culture.* New York: Alfred A. Knopf.

Goldschmidt, D. 1960. *Haggadah Shel Pesach.* Jerusalem.

Goswami, T. n.d. *Āsiŕbbād.* Jorhat: Dhalarsatra Press.

Gray, G. B. 1925. *Sacrifice in the Old Testament. Its Theory and Practice.* Oxford: Clarendon Press.

Griaule, M. 1976. Remarques sur le méchanisme du sacrifice dogon (Soudan français). In de Heusch (ed.), *q.v.*

Harris, G. G. 1978. *Casting out Anger.* Cambridge: Cambridge University Press.

Harris, Marvin. 1978. *Cannibals and Kings: The Origins of Cultures*. London: Collins.

Hayward, C. T. R. 1979. The holy name of the God of Moses and the Prologue of St. John's Gospel. *New Testament Studies* **25** (1), 16—32.

Hermisson, H.-J. 1965. *Sprache und Ritus im altisraelitischen Kult*. Neukirchen-Vluyn: Wageningen.

Herrenschmidt, O. 1978. A qui profite le crime? Cherchez le Sacrifiant: un désir fatalement meurtrier. *L'Homme* **18** (1—2), 7—18.

de Heusch, L. 1976a. Introduction—pour une nouvelle problématique du sacrifice. In de Heusch (ed.) *q.v.*

—— 1976b. Le sacrifice dogon ou la violence de Dieu. In de Heusch (ed.), *q.v.*

—— (ed.) 1976. *Systèmes de pensée en Afrique noire: Le Sacrifice I*. Ivry: C.N.R.S.

Hubert, H. and Mauss, M. 1899. Essai sur la nature et la fonction du sacrifice. *L'Anneé sociologique*, **2**. (Trans. 1964. *Sacrifice, its Nature and Function*. London: Cohen and West.)

Hunter, R. G. 1965. *Shakespeare and the Comedy of Forgiveness*. New York and London: Columbia University Press.

James, E. O. 1920. Sacrifice: introductory and primitive. In *Encyclopedia of Religion and Ethics* (ed.) J. Hastings. Edinburgh.

—— 1933. *The origins of Sacrifice*. London: John Murray.

Jaubert, A. 1963. *La Notion d'Alliance dans le Judaïsme*. Paris.

Jeremias, J. 1966. *The Eucharistic Words of Jesus* (2nd ed.) London: S.C.M. Press.

—— 1972. *New Testament Theology* 1. London: S.C.M. Press.

Kaufmann, Y. 1963. *Tol^edot ha^emunah Hayisraelite, 1—3*. Jerusalem.

Knight, G. Wilson 1930. *Measure for Measure* and the gospels. In *The Wheel of Fire*. London: Oxford University Press.

Kummel, W. G. 1974. *The Theology of the New Testament*. London: S.C.M. Press.

Kuper, H. 1947. *An African Aristocracy: Rank among the Swazi*. London, etc.: Oxford University Press.

Ladd, J. 1957. *The Structure of a Moral Code*. Cambridge, Mass.: Harvard University Press.

Lash, N. 1968. *His Presence in the World: A Study of Eucharistic Worship and Theology*. London: Sheed and Ward.

Leach, E. R. 1964. Magic. In *Dictionary of the Social Sciences* (ed.) J. Goulde and W. Kolbe. London: Tavistock.

—— 1968a Ritual. In *International Encyclopedia of Social Sciences*. New York: MacMillan.

—— 1968b. *A Runaway World?* London: BBC.

—— 1972. The structure of symbolism. In *The Interpretation of Ritual* (ed.) J. S. La Fontaine. London: Tavistock Publications.

—— 1976. *Culture and Communication*. Cambridge: Cambridge University Press.

Leavis, F. R. 1942. The greatness of *Measure for Measure*. *Scrutiny*, **0**, 234–47.

Le Déaut, R. 1961. Le Targum de *Gen.* 22, 8 et I Peter 1, 20. *Recherches de Science Religieuse* **49** (1), 103—6.

—— 1962. Le titre de *Summus Sacerdos* donné à Melchisédech est-il d'origine juive? *Recherches de Science Religieuse* **50** (2), 222—9.

—— 1963. *La Nuit Pascale*. Rome: Pontifical Biblical Institute.

Lévi, I. 1912. Le sacrifice d'Isaac et la mort de Jésus. *Revue des Études Juives* **64**, 171—9.

Lévi-Strauss, C. 1960. On manipulated social models. *Bijdragen Tot de Taal-, Lande-, en Volkenkunde* **116** (1), 45—54.

Lienhardt, R. G. 1961. *Divinity and Experience: The Religion of the Dinka*. Oxford: Clarendon Press.

Lohse, E. 1976. *Die Offenbarung des Johannes*. Göttingen: Vandenhoeck and Ruprecht.

Lukes, S. 1975. *Emile Durkheim, His Life and Work: a Historical and Critical Study*. Harmondsworth: Peregrine Books.

McCarthy, D. J. 1963. *Treaty and Covenant*. (*Analecta Biblica* **21**) Rome: Pontifical Biblical Institute.

—— 1972. *Old Testament Covenant: A Survey of Current Opinions*. Oxford: Blackwell.

McKelvey, R. J. 1969. *The New Temple*. London: Oxford University Press.

MacKinnon, D. M. 1974. *The Problem of Metaphysics*. Cambridge: Cambridge University Press.

Madhavadeva 1957. *Nam-ghosha* (ed.) Haramohan Das. Vrindaban: Vaishnava Theological University.

Maier, J. 1972. *Geschichte der judischen Religion*. Berlin and New York: Walter de Gruyter.

Malinowski, B. 1948. *Magic, Science and Religion, and other essays*. Boston: Beacon Press.

Mascall, E. R. 1953. *Corpus Christi: The Church and the Eucharist*. London, etc.: Longmans.

Masure, E. 1932. *Le Sacrifice du Chef*. Paris. (Trans. 1944. *The Christian Sacrifice*. London: Burnes Oates and Washbourne.)

Mayer, A. C. In press. Public service and individual merit in a town of central India. In *Culture and Morality* (ed.) A. C. Mayer.

Middleton, J. 1960. *Lugbara Religion*. London: Oxford University Press.

Milgrom, J. 1976. Korbān, B. In *Entsyklopedia Miqrait*, 7. Jerusalem.

Moerman, D. E. 1979. Anthropology and symbolic healing. *Current Anthropology* **20** (1), 59—80.

Moule, C. F. D. 1956. *The Sacrifice of Christ*. London: Hodder and Stoughton.

Neog, D. 1963. *Jagat-guru Śaṅkardew*. Nowgong: Srimanta Sankar Mission.

Neog, M. 1965. *Śaṅkaradeva and His Times*. Gauhati: Gauhati University Press.

Nicholson, E. W. 1973. *Exodus and Sinai in History and Tradition*. Oxford: Blackwell.

Pannenberg, W. 1976. *Theology and the Philosophy of Science*. London: Darton, Longman and Todd.

Parry, J. 1974. Egalitarian values in a hierarchical society. *South Asian Review* **7** (2), 95–121.

—— In press. *Ghosts, greed and sin: the occupational identity of the Benares funeral priests*.

Piault, M.-H. 1975. Le miel du pouvoir et le couteau du sacrifice. *L'Homme* **15** (1), 43—61.

Radcliffe-Brown, A. R. 1922. *The Andaman Islanders*. Cambridge: Cambridge University Press.

Radzinowicz, L. 1948. *A History of English Criminal Law and its Administration from 1750, 1*. London: Stevens and Sons.

Redfield, R. 1962. *Human Nature and the Study of Society: the Papers of Robert Redfield, 1*. Chicago: University of Chicago Press.

Rendtorff, R. 1967. *Studien sur Geschichte des Opfers im alten Israel*. Neukirchen-Vluyn: Neukirchener Verlag.

Rogerson, J. W. 1977. The Old Testament view of nature: some preliminary questions. In *Instruction and Interpretation (Oudtestamentlische Studien* **20**) (ed.) A. S. van der Woude. Leiden: Brill.

—— 1978. *Anthropology and the Old Testament*. Oxford: Basil Blackwell.

Rosenbaum, M. and A. M. Silberman 1944. *Pentateuch, with Targum Onkelos, Haphtaroth and Prayers for Sabbath and Rashi's Commentary*. London: Shapiro, Valentine and Company.

Saggs, H. W. F. 1978. *The Encounter with the Divine in Mesopotamia and Israel*. London: Athlone Press.

Sahlins, M. 1978. Culture as protein and profit. *New York Review of Books* **25** (18, 45—53).

Sarma, S. N. 1966. *The neo-Vaisnavite Movement and the Satra Institution of Assam*. Gauhati: Gauhati University Press.

Schweitzer, A. 1951. *Indian Thought and its Development* (trans.) C. E. B. Russell. London: Black.

Segundo, J. 1974. *The Sacraments Today (A Theology for artisans of a New Humanity*, 4). (Trans.) Maryknoll (New York): Orbis Books.

Smart, N. 1972. *The Concept of Worship*. London: MacMillan.

Smith, W. Robertson 1889. *Lectures on the Religion of the Semites*. London: A. and C. Black. (1927: 3rd ed.)

Snaith, N. H. 1967. *Leviticus* and *Numbers*. (*New Century Bible*.) London: Nelson.

Southwold, M. 1978. Buddhism and the definition of religion. *Man* (n.s.) **13** (3), 362—79.

Spiegel, S. 1967. *The Last Trial*. New York: Pantheon Books.

Stephan, H. 1960. *Geschichte der deutschen evangelischen Theologie seit dem deutschen Idealismus*. (2nd ed.) Berlin: A. Töpelmann.

Tempels, P. 1959. *Bantu Philosophy* (trans.). Paris: Présence Africaine.

Turner, V. W. 1962. *Chihamba, The White Spirit: A Ritual Drama of the Ndembu* (Rhodes-Livingstone Papers, 33). Manchester: Manchester University Press.

—— 1966. Colour classification in Ndembu ritual. In *Anthropological Approaches to the Study of Religion* (ed.) Michael Banton. London, etc.: Tavistock.

—— 1967. *Forest of Symbols*. Ithaca and London: Cornell University Press.

—— 1968. *Drums of Affliction*. Oxford: Clarendon Press.

—— 1977. Sacrifice as quintessential process: prophylaxis or abandonment? *History of Religions* **16** (3), 189–215.

Tylor, E. B. 1871. *Primitive Culture*. London.

Van Baal, J. 1975. Offering, sacrifice and gift. *Numen* **23** (3), 161—78.

van Baaren, T. P. 1964. Theoretical speculations on Sacrifice. *Numen* **11** (1), 1—12.

Van der Veen, K. W. 1972. *I Give Thee My Daughter* (trans.) Nanette Jackin. Assen: van Gorcun.

de Vaux, R. 1964. *Studies in Old Testament Sacrifice*. Cardiff: Wales University Press.

Vermes, G. 1970. Bible and Midrash: Early Old Testament exegesis. In *Cambridge History of the Bible, 1*. Cambridge: Cambridge University Press

—— 1973a. *Jesus the Jew*. London: Collins.

—— 1973b. Redemption and Genesis xxii. In *Scripture and Tradition in Judaism* (2nd ed.). Leiden: E. J. Brill.

Weber, M. 1966. *The Sociology of Religion*. London: Methuen (first published 1920—21).

Wellhausen, J. 1878. *Prolegomena zur Geschichte Israels*. Berlin.

Wendland, H. D. 1960. Opfer, III, Im NT. In *Die Religion in Geschichte und Gegenwart* 4. Tubingen.

West, M. 1975. The Shades come to Town: ancestors and urban independent churches. In *Religion and Social Change in Southern Africa* (ed.) M. Whisson and M. West. Cape Town: David Philip.

Westermarck, E. 1906. *The Origin and Development of Moral Ideas, 1*, London: MacMillan.

—— 1908. Ib., vol. 2.

—— 1932. *Ethical Relativity*. London: Kegan Paul and Co.

Wiles, F. M. 1974. *The Remaking of Christian Doctrine*. London: S. C. M. Press.

Wilson, M. 1957. *Rituals of Kinship among the Nyakyusa*. London: Oxford University Press.

Yadin, Y. 1977. *Megillat Haqodesh, 1*. Jerusalem.

Young, F. M. 1975. *Sacrifice and the Death of Christ*. London: S.P.C.K.

AUTHOR INDEX